eCom MasterPlan

YOUR 3 STEPS TO SUCCESSFUL
ONLINE SELLING

Chloë **Thomas**

© Copyright Chloë Thomas, 2013

Published 2013

Kernu Publishing

Windsor House

12–14 High Street

Kidlington

OX5 2DH

United Kingdom

ISBN 978-0-9573128-5-2

Cover photograph: © Jacqueline Cross Photographer
www.jacquelinecrossphotography.com

Cover and interior design: Visual Philosophy Ltd
www.VisualPhilosophy.com

Illustrations: Joni McPherson, McPherson Graphics
www.McPhersonGraphics.com

Printed in the United Kingdom by TJ International, Cornwall, UK

Praise For *eCommerce MasterPlan 1.8*

....

'Chloë has done the impossible – condensed a massively complex and detailed subject into a crisp clear set of "To do" lists with masses of live examples. I tried very hard, but could not find anything she had left out.

Anyone running an eCommerce business will relate to so much of this book and get the inspiration to get on and improve their business almost immediately.

In 12 years of running an eCommerce business, I have found that just as you crack one new method of digital marketing, two more grow in its place. This book seems to get a grip of all the methods and allows you to conquer them in a manageable way.

If you are just starting on the eCommerce route, congratulations, you have found the Bible – I suggest you read Step 2, Chapter 4 (Building the Right Website) very thoroughly, right now!'

Mark Ashley Miller, Founder, The Present Finder

'This is the Bible to Website Management and Marketing 101. A good bookshelf addition for all dot.com dinosaurs, successful online managers, web entrepreneurs or total novices who need a no-nonsense straight-to-the-point read of where to start and how.

I myself have been in this industry now for 12 years and it's always good to go back to the basics and refresh your own learning – that's why I love this book.

Chloë Thomas shows you step by step how to build and manage your online business. She strips back to the core of what you are trying to achieve and demonstrates that it takes work, but it's much easier than you thought. Easy and enjoyable to read, with a clear plan of action and totally applicable to today.'

Maxine Duncan, Online Commercial Manager, La Senza UK

'eCommerce can be a minefield of abbreviations, technical terms and (like IT) a complex journey that would scare most people off creating and marketing a website.

The *eCommerce MasterPlan* by Chloë, an experienced eCommerce professional, breaks down many of the uncertainties of the eCommerce world. Understanding your business model as identified in Step 1 is key, and following the simple worksheets will really set you up for success and help you to plan properly.

Throughout the *eCommerce MasterPlan*, relevance is put on the importance of content being King. Plus, one small step that is planned is better than jumping in feet first with multiple ideas that don't get the attention needed. Chloë has also laid bare the fundamentals of running a website, going out to tender with documents to make life easier and the key components of driving traffic to a website.

This book has something for everyone, whether a novice entering the world of eCommerce or someone like myself who has worked in eCommerce for many years. There is a takeaway for everyone.

This eCommerce master class not only covers the core elements you would expect, but goes one step further highlighting how to work out ROI, and giving simple examples that actually make sense. Plus, it's packed with ideas that you will be able to apply to your everyday planning, implementation and review of digital marketing.

A great read and followed up by a training course that will keep your mind bubbling for hours to come.'

Lee Carpenter-Johnson, eCommerce Director, Galactic Online

'The *eCommerce MasterPlan* provides a useful roadmap for what is still a relatively new industry. The MasterPlan contains a first step to assist the reader in identifying their type of business and removes any concern of a "one size fits all" approach. The author has used her broad experience to provide a book giving the sort of specialised advice normally only available with large-scale consulting spend.

This book is a must-read for anyone looking to build on their eCommerce efforts. The added content online gives the reader the chance to work examples and complete workbooks, as well as the comfort that this is as up to date as the author's impressive knowledge base.'

Penny Cuthbert, Project Manager, Tesco.com

'In this book, Chloë sets out to aid you to write and deliver your very own eCommerce business MasterPlan and she does this in spades. From the cerebral to the extremely practical, you won't be short of a simple action list, which, when implemented, will deliver you a cast-iron ROI.'

James Aston, Managing Director, Moneyspyder Ltd

Thank You!

. . . .

The *eCommerce MasterPlan* (*eCMP*) journey began in May and was launched in September 2012. Since then, I've been amazed by the response the *eCMP* message has received – there are businesses large and small out there using it to help them build their success. Several businesses have come to events I've been running and speaking at to accelerate their progress further – thank you to everyone who's given me feedback so far and in the future!

My team at indiumonline are, quite frankly, awesome, so thank you all for looking after our great clients while I have been immersed in all things *eCMP*!

Thank you to Sue Richardson and her team for making the publishing process so easy and straightforward. Thank you to Chantal Cooke for getting the *eCMP* message into lots of papers, magazines and more. As ever, a big thank you to Paul Avins, my F10 buddies and all the Business Wealth Club community for all your help, advice and support.

Finally, I would like to say a massive thank you to Mum, Dad, Rob & Alice, Will and all my family and friends.

Thank you.

Chloë Thomas

July 2013

Contents

. . . .

Not all eCommerce businesses are the same, and not all
successful eCommerce businesses are the same. However,
all the successful ones do fit into similar moulds. By
consciously building your business based on one of these
structures, you will build a better business faster.

As well as fitting into one of the seven eCommerce Business
Structures, the strongest eCommerce performers usually
have a product range that is at one end of the Product Range
Scale.

Chapter 3: Differentiating Your Business 31

You need to understand how you're competing with the competition and what you're going to do to stand out. This means identifying your generic strategy and defining your Unique Selling Point (USP).

Step 2: Establishing the Core Foundations 41

Chapter 4: Building the Right Website 43

The website is the most important part of any eCommerce business. What sort of website do you need? How do you build it quickly and effectively? How do you find the right PiggyBack website? Plus, how can you avoid conversion blockers?

Chapter 5: Building Your Business for Profit and Growth 69

To build the basis for future profit and growth, you need to get a handle on the key numbers in an eCommerce business. That is, the overheads, the margin and the return on investment (ROI). Then you will know what you need to achieve.

Chapter 6: Selecting Your Products and Promotions 87

Once you know the numbers, you can start organising what your products are going to be, and promotions sit very closely with your product decisions. How many products do you need? What promotions are you going to run? What mix do you need?

Step 3: I Have Built It: Why Haven't They Come? (aka Marketing!)

It's the marketing plan that will bring you your customers and make them spend. Here, we go through how to take the outcomes of the other 2 Steps and build them into a marketing plan.

Chapter 7: Researching Your Marketing Plan

To create a great marketing plan you need to research what should go into it – what's happening inside and outside your business.

Chapter 8: Creating Your Marketing Plan

Your marketing plan pulls together everything covered in the book so far.

Chapter 9: Test, Measure and Optimise Your Marketing

Marketing requires constant testing, measuring and optimising. What do you need to be aware of when you're doing this? Attribution, segmentation and more…

You've Read the Book, What's Next?

Recommended Reading

Introduction

. . . .

What is eCommerce?

When I talk about eCommerce, I mean:

- a business
- selling products or services
- taking the order online

So, it could be a business selling thousands of books per month, it could be a travel agency or even a kids' party entertainer who takes bookings online.

eCommerce also needn't be the whole business. There are many eCommerce businesses with a wholesale division on the side. There are many 'offline' businesses with an eCommerce area. Just look at *eCommerce MasterPlan* – some of our products and services you can buy online, others you have to buy face to face or over the phone.

Why an *eCommerce* *MasterPlan*?

eCommerce is a huge, growing industry. In the UK in 2012, eCommerce grew by 16%, whilst Europe remains the biggest eCommerce marketplace. North America is catching up, and the eCommerce market in the Middle East grew by 45% in 2012.

Despite its size and maturity (in some markets), there is no roadmap for success. There is no easy-to-follow guide that will help eCommerce businesses succeed. I find it highly frustrating seeing great businesses wasting opportunities in eCommerce, and wasting time on the wrong marketing and the wrong website just because they haven't the luxury of the time to research the other options. It's that wasted time, effort and money that I hope *eCommerce MasterPlan* will help many businesses to avoid.

What is *eCommerce* *MasterPlan* Based On?

Since 2001, I have been working in direct marketing and, since 2004, I have been directly involved with the structures and marketing of eCommerce businesses. At the last count, I have been directly involved with the marketing of over 50 eCommerce businesses, some as a member of staff and some as a consultant. I have project managed more than 15 eCommerce website builds or rebuilds, and advised on many more. I have helped eCommerce businesses launch and go international, and have also helped high-street retailers launch online.

Unfortunately, I have also seen eCommerce businesses close or go under, simply because they didn't understand what sort of businesses they were, used the wrong marketing or invested in the wrong website. All are issues that are possible to avoid.

The businesses I've work for have sold everything from high-street fashion, to books, to holidays, to workshops and downloads. In all that time, I have barely seen two businesses approach eCommerce in the same way. All have done some things well, all have done some things badly – teams, structure, products, websites. Almost every business I've looked at is avoiding a marketing method that holds a key to their success, or stubbornly holding on to one that is doing them no favours at all.

What I have learnt along the way is that there are some clear structures that, when followed, invariably lead to success, and some great big potholes that, if you know about them in advance, are really easy to avoid.

eCommerce MasterPlan is based on all I have learnt from spending my working life immersed in eCommerce. I believe it provides the blueprint, the roadmap, the master plan for the success of every eCommerce business. If you follow the 3 Steps outlined in this book, you will build an eCommerce business that succeeds. And you will get there faster. (If you want to get there really fast, then read the other two books in this series as well! Find them here **eCommerceMasterPlan.com/books**)

The 3 Steps are based on the thousands of conversations I have had with eCommerce business owners about the problems and successes they are having at all stages of the business lifecycle. These are conversations with people who either:

- have a successful business, but want to take it to the next level

- have a great idea for an eCommerce business, but can't work out where or how to start
- have a business that should be doing well, but just doesn't seem to be taking off in the way it could
- are selling lots on Amazon or eBay and want to grow direct sales via their own website.

If you are reading this book, you are almost certainly in one of those positions yourself and this book will help you to get started, avoid the pitfalls and take your business to the next level.

The *eCommerce MasterPlan* in Under 250 Words

. . . .

Put simply, *eCommerce MasterPlan* is a three-step plan that will show you your recipe for success.

Step 1

One of the fundamental problems I see again and again with eCommerce businesses is that they don't know what they are trying to be.

There are just seven eCommerce Business Structures: by the end of Step 1 you will know which one you are. You will also identify your Unique Selling Point (USP) and your Product Range Scale (PRS) – once you know these three things, building your MasterPlan is simple.

Step 2

To be successful at the heart of your eCommerce business, you need to do three things well: create the perfect website; understand the numbers behind the profit; and manage your products and promotions to keep your customers engaged.

In Step 2, you'll learn how to build these and keep them working well for you. Get them right and the rest will be easy.

Step 3

Step 1 identifies what sort of eCommerce business you are; this will help to identify what type of marketing is going to work for you. Step 2 builds the foundation of the business ready for sales – and marketing is going to bring the traffic that drives the sales to you.

Step 3 will show you how to build your marketing plan, what should be in it and how to optimise it to keep the magic happening.

How to Use this Book

. . . .

At the heart of the *eCommerce MasterPlan* is an understanding of what sort of eCommerce business you are running; so reading the first section and getting to grips with Step 1 is really rather critical.

After that, if you're an established eCommerce business, then you can get away with skipping to Step 3 to understand what the essential marketing methods for your type of eCommerce business are. But, at some point, please do read Step 2 as you will learn vitally useful information to help you grow your business.

If you are new to eCommerce, then I highly recommend that you read through all the Steps in order before starting to implement.

Once you have worked through the key areas for you, then the whole book is structured so you can easily dip into the right part for you when you need it.

eCommerce and online marketing are constantly changing, so I've designed the book to help you take the right approach no matter what changes. Of course, though, you need to keep up to date with what's happening and how to use each of the tools: that's where **eCommerceMasterPlan.com** comes in, and throughout the book you'll find the following symbols when there's useful content available for you online:

WORKBOOK

I have created a series of workbooks to help you make the most of each section – so make sure you download them to work through alongside the sections. If you want to get the workbook for the whole book right now, then just go to **eCommerceMasterPlan.com/Free**

DOWNLOAD...

I have also put a lot of useful templates on the website ready for you to download and use. Please do make the most of these when you see this logo.

WEBSITE

When there's some great extra content that will help you on the website, we've used this logo.

Enjoy!

What Sort of eCommerce Business Are You?
- Identify your eCommerce Business Structure
- Identify the Scale of Your Product Range
- Differentiate your Business

Establishing The Core Foundations
- Build the Right Website
- Build your Business for Profit and Growth
- Select your Products and Promotions

I Have Built It: Why haven't they come? (aka Marketing!)
- Research your Marketing Plan
- Creating your Marketing Plan
- Test, Measure and Optimise your Marketing

The first step in building your eCommerce MasterPlan is to understand what sort of business you are building.

By the end of this step, you will know the answer to the three questions that sit at the heart of any eCommerce business:

- **What is your eCommerce Business Structure?**
- **What is the Scale of your Product Range?**
- **What differentiates your business? What is your Unique Selling Point (USP)?**

The answers to these three questions will impact on everything you do with your business, from systems, to products, to customer service and marketing.

WORKBOOK

You can download the workbook for Step 1 or each individual chapter at **eCommerceMasterPlan.com/Free**

CHAPTER 1

Identifying your eCommerce Business Structure

Not all eCommerce businesses are the same, and not all successful eCommerce businesses are the same. However, all the successful ones do fit into similar moulds. By consciously building your business based on one of these structures, you will build a better business faster.

The structures are defined by how customers can browse, learn about and purchase your products – aka your routes to market. There are four ways that customers can see your products and buy them:

- **Your own website** – this includes mobile sites.

- **A catalogue** – a catalogue is a paper mailing of at least four pages, sent to a defined list (of customers or prospective customers), that includes all the product information details and product prices so customers can place their order straight away, without going elsewhere for more information. Think Argos, Boden or Scotts of Stow.

- **Your stores/stalls** – a physical shop where customers come to you, browse the items and buy them. If you only do one show a year, or a pop-up shop at Christmas, consider your stores/stalls a marketing method and don't use them to decide on your eCommerce Business Structure.

- **Via someone else's website** – if you display your products on Amazon, eBay, Not On the High Street, Etsy or similar, you're 'PiggyBacking' on their technology and customer database to get the sales in.

You'll notice there's no mention of call centres so far, or of taking orders by phone. For customer service reasons, ANY eCommerce business should be ready and willing to take a call from a customer and an order over the phone if necessary. So it's not (and shouldn't be) a separate factor in defining which business structure you have.

. . . .

The Seven eCommerce Business Structures

Successful eCommerce businesses understand which of the seven eCommerce Business Structures they are in and build their businesses around that understanding.

If your eCommerce business is to be really successful, you need to embrace your eCommerce Business Structure. Over the years, your business structure may progress – so you may start on a Niche PiggyBack structure, move to an Online Only, and finally a Boutique Bricks and Clicks.

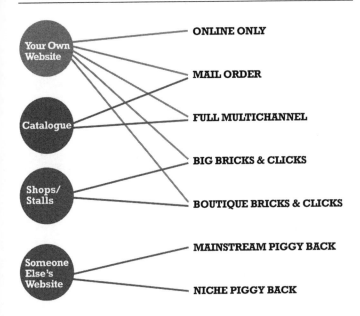

To help you understand the separate eCommerce Business Structures, we've explained each below with an example plus the key challenges for businesses that have that structure.

Online Only

A business where the only route to purchase is online is the most straightforward of our structures. There are no catalogue mailings to new or existing customers, and no physical store for people to buy in either. But the business does take orders over the phone.

Examples: asos.com, lookfantastic.com, Made.com.

Biggest challenge for the Online Only eCommerce business:
- Customer recruitment and growth.

Mail Order

This is a business where a key part of the sales is driven by catalogue mailings. There is a transactional website plus a printed catalogue, and possibly one or two physical stores usually at the warehouse and/or call centre.

Examples: Boden, House of Bath, Lands' End.

Biggest challenges for the Mail Order eCommerce business:
- Understanding the joint role of catalogues and online marketing to bring customers to the business.
- Getting customers to order via the website (usually much more cost effective for the business).

Bricks and Clicks

Bricks and Clicks is any business that has physical stores as well as its eCommerce website, but has no mailing catalogue. These could be high-street stores, retail park stores, or stores in obscure locations, but they must be physical locations in which consumers can buy the products. This also includes travelling stores, if you're a market trader or attend many shows and craft fairs each year.

There is a lot of diversity among this group, so we've split them into two sections. When a business goes from having one or two shops to having more than that, the systems and structures for the business fundamentally change. To take account of this, we have divided these eCommerce Bricks and Clicks businesses into those with three or more stores (Big Bricks and Clicks), and those with only one or two (Boutique Bricks and Clicks).

Big Bricks and Clicks

Big Bricks and Clicks are companies with chains of stores (three or more stores) – either regionally or nationally.

For these businesses, the shop has almost always come before the website, so there will have been put in place some proper structure for creating processes for the fulfilment of online orders and for the creation of the product information around which to build the website (in a shop you rarely need a picture of the item, or a written description of it).

Example: Argos, Boots, Topshop, House of Fraser.

Biggest challenge for the Big Bricks and Clicks eCommerce business:
- Fully integrating the stores and website – people and systems.

Boutique Bricks and Clicks

Boutique Bricks and Clicks are companies with one or two physical locations, usually regionally deployed.

Sometimes these businesses start with a shop and then decide to sell online as well, but for many of them it has happened the other way round!

The successful ones are usually businesses focused on a clear niche, be it a clothing boutique with a certain style or a haberdashery store. So, usually, they sell something that is hard to find.

Example: BrownsFashion.com, Home and Pantry (Islington), ecco Oxford, Truro Fabrics.

Biggest challenge for the Boutique Bricks and Clicks eCommerce business:

- Keeping the physical shop and online shop up to date and consistent with each other – it's a tough juggling act, especially at the beginning when sales are low.

PiggyBacking

As with the Bricks and Clicks eCommerce businesses, we've divided this sector into two (Mainstream PiggyBacking and Niche PiggyBacking).

PiggyBacking is the use of someone else's infrastructure to get your products to market. That infrastructure usually includes:

- website and payment system
- marketing
- brand awareness
- customer database

This leaves the PiggyBacking business 'only' having to find the products and process the orders.

The benefits to the eCommerce business can be huge:

- Speed – you can get your products in front of prospective buyers within minutes, and be generating sales within hours.
- Investment – you don't need to build a website or a payment system – so the set-up costs are negligible.
- Legal – all the legal faff of selling online is dealt with by the company whose site you are PiggyBacking (for example, PCI DSS, Cookie Laws, 3D Secure, etc.).

Possibly the biggest benefit is that you can use this system to build and test your business. You can work out what sells, and at what price, and you can build up a customer database ready for when you go out on your own.

But there are big risks too – if you fall out with the company you're PiggyBacking on, that's your business dead overnight.

Mainstream PiggyBacking

This is using sites like Amazon and eBay, where you are tapping into their huge infrastructure and customer base.

You can sell pretty much anything through these organisations and you don't need your own website at all.

Biggest challenge for the Mainstream PiggyBack eCommerce business:

- Deciding when/if you should create your own website (and finding the time to do it)!

Niche PiggyBacking

Niche PiggyBacking is where sellers of similar products come together to market more easily, usually retaining their own blog or eCommerce site elsewhere too. Examples include the craft world (Etsy, Folksy), hotels (Hotels.com, LateRooms.com), jewellery (Boticca) and books (AbeBooks.co.uk).

Rather than getting you in front of the world, these niche businesses get you in front of segments of consumers who want your products.

Usually, in these Niche PiggyBacking arrangements, the consumer's visibility of you as the seller is far greater – so it's more obvious that they are buying from you, not from the site you are PiggyBacking.

In most cases, you'll also want your own website, because the products you are selling gain in value depending on the amount of information you are able to provide to the consumer. So, if you are an Etsy seller, you will want to have your own blog with more information about what you do and examples of previous work and new projects. If you are a hotel, you will want your own website to answer the questions you can't fit into the LateRooms.com formats.

In addition, many Niche PiggyBackers will also be selling via Amazon and eBay.

Biggest challenges for the Niche PiggyBack eCommerce business:
- Building a good reputation on the Niche PiggyBack site.
- Choosing the right site to PiggyBack on.

Full Multichannel

Multichannel is the merger of Mail Order and Bricks and Clicks: a business that has a catalogue, a website and stores. It can also include PiggyBacking. This is by far the most difficult to succeed at because each of the three channels has different demands:

- In a catalogue the prices are printed, so you are stuck with them for some time – one month, three months, perhaps even a year. In retail, you can change prices overnight – launch a sale or a new promotion, etc. Online, you can launch a promotion in seconds.
- In a catalogue you state several hundred products that are available to buy over a period of time. If the stock doesn't come in, you have issues. In retail and online, you simply remove the product.
- You have got stock in lots of places – how do you integrate this?
- There are very few systems that do all three channels well – you are likely to end up compromising.
- Customer service can be a real issue, and customer expectations keep getting higher.

Many retail businesses have failed because they decided to be Multichannel but got it wrong. Few businesses have succeeded in becoming true Multichannel.

Example: Bravissimo, Next, Screwfix, Crew Clothing.

Biggest challenge for the Multichannel eCommerce business:
- Keeping the needs of customers across the channels satisfied – building a seamless experience.

Extra Complexities – Frequently Asked Questions about Selecting Your eCommerce Business Structure

Wholesale

Wholesale means selling products in bulk to other businesses, which then sell the product on to the consumers. For the purposes of working out your eCommerce Business Structure, you should ignore your wholesale division.

Preview Sale Sites/Members Only eCommerce Sites

These are the websites where you need to register and then you get alerted to each special sale. These sales are usually only for a few days and focus on a certain product range/brand for the duration.

These are just another form of online selling, not another eCommerce Business Structure. So, if you are one, then choose your eCommerce Business Structure based on your routes to market. If you sell via them, you're PiggyBacking on them!

PLUS+PiggyBack

According to Hitwise, over 30% of all traffic to eCommerce websites in the UK goes to either Amazon or eBay. So, if you want to get in front of certain consumers, you need to be on those websites. There are now many Online Only, Mail Order, etc. businesses trying out PiggyBacking as another route to market. Plus lots of PiggyBacking businesses trying out building their direct sales via a website.

If you're one of those businesses, then select your eCommerce Business Structure based on where the majority of your sales come from. This might seem like a cop out, but it really isn't! Let me explain why:

- If you already have an eCommerce business and you're testing out PiggyBacking, the only areas of your business it will affect are the IT systems and customer services – so it doesn't make a big difference to how you structure your business as long as you get the integrations right.
- If you're a PiggyBacker building your own website, you have those system changes to make, but also a marketing function to get active with (so definitely read Step 3). However, until your own site takes more than the PiggyBacking, you should continue to use that eCommerce Business Structure.

······································

Chapter 1 Complete: What's Next?

Settling on your eCommerce Business Structure is the most important decision you can make in an eCommerce business. It influences every single area of the business – so be confident in your choice and stick to it!

NOTES

What are the key points from this section?

_____

_____

_____

My eCommerce Business Structure is:

_____

_____

_____

_____

_____

Other notes:

_____

_____

_____

_____

_____

_____

WEBSITE
Visit **eCommerceMasterPlan.com** for more information on the seven eCommerce Business Structures.

CHAPTER 2
Identifying the Scale of Your Product Range

As well as fitting into one of the seven eCommerce Business Structures, the strongest eCommerce performers usually have a product range that is at one end of the Product Range Scale (PRS).

Niche

Department Store

The PRS isn't anything to do with the number of products you sell; it's about how varied those products are.

At the Niche End of the Scale

Niche sellers focus on a single product category – tea towels, sailing holidays, ladies' shoes – and they create and edit the perfect range of that product in such a way that, if you want that product, you know they are the only seller to go to, e.g. Classic-Sailing.co.uk, TheVacuumBagShop.co.uk, BatteryStation.co.uk, ToDryFor.com.

Compatible eCommerce Business Structures:
- All of them!

See the end of this chapter and the website for examples and case studies of niche PRS companies.

. . . .

At the Department Store End of the Scale

Department store sellers stock EVERYTHING. Like a traditional high-street department store, their website is packed with all kinds of different products, but even more products than the traditional department stores could ever possibly stock. So, John Lewis is less of an online department store than Tesco, Amazon or Next. The aim of firms at this end of the scale is to become their customers' go-to destination every time those customers think of buying online.

Compatible eCommerce Business Structures:

- Online Only
- Mail Order
- Big Bricks and Clicks
- Full Multichannel

. . . .

In the Middle of the PRS

The businesses in the middle, therefore, are not the obvious place for the consumer to go to for what they want. They are neither the default 'I bet Amazon has it' choice, nor are they likely to come up when someone searches for their product.

To be successful here, you need to build and retain a good loyal customer base and a strong brand that ties all the product types together.

Compatible eCommerce Business Structures:
- Boutique Bricks and Clicks
- Bricks and Clicks
- Mail Order
- Full Multichannel
- Mainstream PiggyBacking
- Niche PiggyBacking

. . . .

Why is it Important?

To be successful anywhere but at the niche end, you need to either have a very strong brand or a massive customer base.

It is so much easier to be successful at the niche end for several important reasons. Having a select group of products:

- makes it easy for customers to understand your business – if they understand you, they'll remember you, recommend you and come back again
- makes it easy for you to build great internal skills in buying that product type
- spreads your cash less far – if you only stock X, then you don't have to fund so many product lines
- makes your marketing easier – one consistent message
- makes it easier to build up lots of content and PR because you can easily be seen as the experts in that area

- sometimes streamlines pick and pack operations – similar sized and weighted products are really easy
- and much more…

However many products you choose to stock, you should edit those products for your customers – have a basic, better and best of each thing – and nothing more. Consumers really appreciate being helped to find the right option. Plus, it will help you to keep inventory down.

At either end of the scale, your strategic plan is fairly straightforward: every decision you make is tailored towards seeing how well it fits with your overall proposition. However, it's VERY hard to start off as a department store. These eCommerce businesses have taken their PRS wide in order to maximise their customer base and brand power – so it's almost impossible to enter the market here.

 Top Tip

Don't assume that being niche means you can't be big

One of the fastest-growing eCommerce businesses at the moment is WorldStores, with a turnover of over £35m. WorldStores have built their business on niches. They identify ranges of keywords that have a high search volume with a low amount of competition from other providers, and where they know they can offer a better product range and customer service than the other providers do. For each niche, they build a new website (on a central platform). Currently, they have websites for products as diverse as garden sheds and chimineas, to rowing machines and cots – over 70 websites in all.

Niche Product Range Scale Case Studies

Bravissimo

www.bravissimo.com

In 1995, Sarah Tremellen set up Bravissimo. Bravissimo started with (and still has) a very niche product range: bras in cup sizes D–KK. Therefore, they are very much at the 'niche' end of the PRS, and they really edit their range to make sure that every product they sell is up to standard. The business started as Mail Order, and has now diversified online and into 21 stores around the UK. It fits perfectly into our Multichannel eCommerce Business Structure, and is one firm that has done a good job of integrating the three sales channels. When a customer gets to the till in store, they are asked for their postcode and their customer records are brought up on the till, so the company has a complete view of that customer's interactions with them. Plus, if the item the customer wants isn't in store, it can be posted to them, and customers can ask the call centre to deliver to the store for them as well. So the customer sees a VERY joined-up process.

In 1995, ladies needing these larger cup sizes would enter their local department store lingerie section and ask, 'Do you have anything in my size?', buying what (if anything) was available. Sarah Tremellen's aim was to make it easier for these ladies to find bras that fit, and to have a range of bras to choose from. With her target customers having such a bad experience in the past, it would have been easy to just assume that providing the products would be enough to secure the sales. That hasn't been the Bravissimo approach, though. Their USP isn't the larger bra sizes; it's the customer service: every store has a number of well-proportioned changing rooms, each with a chair and pretty gown, plus several fully-trained bra fitters, who are able to make sure you have got the right size of bra (which can even fix back problems, and make you look 10 times better) and know the whole range inside out – even which brand will suit your shape the best. The in-store experience, together with the product selection and joined-up IT systems, show how Bravissimo has put customer service at the centre of everything they do. It's also enabled them to successfully extend the product range from just underwear into swimwear and, most recently, the spin off clothing label PepperBerry.

Classic Sailing

www.classic-sailing.co.uk

Classic Sailing was founded in 1995 by Adam and Debbie Purser, to 'take people to sea for safe sailing adventures'. It has a very niche range of products: sailing courses and one-to-many-night trips as part of the crew of various sailing ships that voyage around the UK and around the world, everywhere from St Mawes in Cornwall to the Antarctic.

As well as being a business with a very niche product range, it has a fairly niche customer base. The business is primarily online, with one mailing per year, so it fits into our Online Only eCommerce Business Structure. The prospective customer base for sailing holidays and courses that Classic Sailing offer is relatively small, so customer retention is essential. The number one reason why someone will book again is because they enjoyed the experience last time, so strong customer service is really important. But it's not the USP.

Classic Sailing's USP is next to impossible for any of their competition to copy and is founded on Adam and Debbie's love of sailing. Even taking a quick look at their website, you can't fail to notice the vast amount of content and the detail of that content. There's almost the full history of each of their sailing vessels, and full guides to the schedules of each boat and each specialist trip. Plus, blog content on every sailing trip the owners go on themselves, and on those the customers go on, too. If you love sailing, it's a site where you can easily lose a Friday afternoon. This knowledge and information has a multitude of benefits: it brings customers back to the site again and again, it builds the Classic Sailing brand, it attracts new customers and it's brilliant for marketing.

Chapter 2 Complete: What's Next?

Defining the scale of your product range and leveraging it to benefit your business is really important in everything you do.

NOTES

What are the key points from this section?

_____

_____

_____

My PRS is:

_____

_____

_____

_____

_____

_____

Other notes:

_____

_____

_____

_____

_____

WEBSITE

Visit **eCommerceMasterPlan.com** for more information on how PRS affects eCommerce businesses.

CHAPTER 3

Differentiating Your Business

Unfortunately, just knowing what you are isn't enough. You need to understand how you're competing with the competition and what you're going to do to stand out. This means identifying your generic strategy and defining your USP. (If you're at the niche end of the Product Range Scale you've got a head start here!)

There are millions of eCommerce websites that your prospective customers can buy from. There are probably hundreds of thousands of eCommerce websites on which they can buy similar products to yours. So you need to create a reason for them to buy from you – and to keep buying from you; something that differentiates you from all the other websites out there (and from the shops and catalogues they could buy from too).

By differentiating yourself, you create a USP for your business – the unique reason why customers will keep buying from you rather than anyone else. For your USP to be effective, you need to be really good at whatever you choose to differentiate in and be better than the competition: you need to be 'best in class'.

Identifying Your Generic Strategy

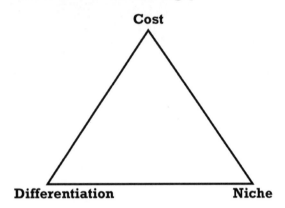

In the 1960s, Michael Porter defined three generic strategies for business:

1 Cost leadership (how in control of your costs you are, which relates directly to how much you charge).
2 Niche/focus (a customer group you will focus on).
3 Differentiation (products).

It is still true today that every business needs to decide on which of these three it will primarily focus on; you will fail if you try to be all things to all. But, in the 21st century, no company can afford to ignore their cost base or misunderstand their core customer base. So a USP needs to be more than just one of these three generic strategies.

Saying this, the three generic strategies above are a good place to start. It's crucial to understand whether any of these is critical in your business sector.

Take a look at your sector. If your sector is full of commodity products – those you can get from lots of places – then it's going to be price sensitive (think TVs, laptops, books and DVDs). The customer goes to the cheapest store to buy. That's really easy online because it's easy to compare lots of the same products in minutes and find the cheapest. If this is the case in your industry, then you're going to struggle unless you spend time reducing your costs so you can price effectively and still make money.

Are you targeting a specialist market? Are you targeting a very tight and closely defined group of customers? Now that we can easily sell globally, even the most specialist market is big enough to have multiple eCommerce sites serving it. In this case, really understanding your customers and what they need and want is going to be everything.

Differentiation – are you bringing something totally new? Does your product solve a never before solved problem? Are you serving customers in a totally new way? This is going to be tough – everything about your business is experimental!

So, which Generic Strategy is going to be successful in your marketplace? Whichever your generic strategy is will impact all your business decisions. However, to attract and keep your customers, you need a further point of differentiation and that is your USP.

Identifying Your USP

Your USP needs to be available in your marketplace. If it isn't, then you have got to be better at the USP than the company currently occupying that space or you won't be unique. Successful differentiation online becomes a competitive game; once you have successfully differentiated your business, expect the competition to follow. You can never rest and believe you have got it completely sorted. Don't be fooled, it's really not easy; it's hard work, it takes time and it's not cheap. But when you succeed, you'll reap the rewards.

Selecting and building on your USP is essential for your success. The USP makes it easy for new and existing customers to 'get' you (just like your Product Range Scale (PRS) in Chapter 2). The quicker a customer can understand what your business stands for, the quicker they'll trust you. And trust = recommendations and repeat purchases + forgiveness when things go a little bit wrong!

The quicker a prospective customer 'gets' you, the sooner and more likely they'll be to buy from you. So the right, clear USP will increase your sales and growth.

The USP is also critical to the internal structure, processes, people and marketing of your business – a clear USP that everyone understands will really drive the business.

What are the Successful eCommerce USPs?

Let me help you fast track identifying your USP.

There are seven USPs that work well in eCommerce. The first three are the most powerful (the hardest for your competition to copy):

- **Customer Service** – this aligns closely with a Delivery and Returns USP, but is much more than getting the parcel out correctly. It's about all the ways you communicate with a customer. You need to be responding within hours (not days) to queries on Facebook, Twitter, email, etc. and you need to make it really easy for customers to do business with you. Going the extra mile is also critical: when one of International Dance Supplies' Greek customer's parcels didn't arrive in time for their dance school show, one of the International Dance Supplies team hopped on a plane with replacements! Are you willing to do that?

- **Knowledge and Information** – this is the value-add over the product. Can the customer be 100% sure that the item on your website is the one they want? Have you included the length of the skirt, the batteries that the MP3 player takes? And it's more than that – do you show customers how to use your products? Videos, articles and guides are all key. Your site needs to be the centre for information on your products.

- **Customer Base** – this is one differentiator that is VERY hard and VERY expensive for your competition to steal. It's also expensive to build; you need a huge list of customers who will consistently buy from you – think Amazon or John Lewis.

- **Brand** – this can be closely linked to building a big customer base. Be front of mind, be the only choice for what you are offering. Own your industry. Online auction = eBay; online bookshop = Amazon; fast fashion = ASOS. At the moment, there aren't many more...

- **Delivery and Returns** – this is a major battleground. Speed, price and reliability are key. In some industries (fashion and hardware/ironmongery), next-day delivery, free if you order by 9pm, is becoming the norm. So to get to those levels you also need to have very good systems in place that keep errors and costs down: real-time stock is a must.

- **Products** – exclusive products and products that are hard to find all play a part here, BUT so does your selection – do the editing for the customer.
- **Price** – in commodity markets, there is still a lot of opportunity in being the cheapest. Just don't forget that you have got to be aware of the delivery costs; your customers will factor those in.

Select and Implement Your Differentiation

Decide which generic strategy is important in your sector – can your business fit with that? If not, what do you need to do to make it fit?

Define your USP – define it in a statement that everyone in your business (and eventually your customers) will quickly remember and understand.

. . . .

Chapter 3 Complete: What's Next?

Once you've selected your USP and generic strategy, stick with them. It takes time (months if not years) to build your point of difference in the mind of the consumer, therefore, you need to stick with your point of difference and not be tempted to change it every few months.

You need to build your USP and generic strategy into everything your business does – the marketing, the systems, the people, the technology. If someone sliced your business in half, this is what they should find; it's what you are.

NOTES

What are the key points from this section?

_____

_____

_____

What is your generic strategy?

_____

_____

_____

_____

What is your USP?

_____

_____

_____

Other notes:

_____

_____

_____

_____

WEBSITE
Visit **eCommerceMasterPlan.com** for more information on differentiation.

Step 1: What Sort of eCommerce Business Are You? Complete: What's Next?

· ·

You should now understand your eCommerce business:

- The eCommerce Business Structure – how you get your products in front of your customers.
- The Product Range Scale – what you're selling.
- Differentiation – your Generic Strategy and your Unique Selling Point – what makes your business different.

As we build the eCommerce MasterPlan for your business, whenever there's an important decision to be made, keep asking yourself:

- **'Does this fit with my eCommerce Business Structure?'**
- **'Does this change my Product Range Scale?'**
- **'Does this support my USP?'**

These three parts of Step 1 will influence every decision in your business, and changing any of them should be a thoroughly thought through decision.

NOTES

What are the key points from Step 1?

_____

_____

_____

_____

My eCommerce Business Structure is:

_____

_____

_____

_____

My PRS is:

_____

_____

_____

_____

My Generic Strategy is:

_____

_____

_____

_____

My USP is:

_____

_____

_____

_____

_____

_____

Other notes:

_____

_____

_____

_____

_____

_____

_____

_____

WEBSITE

Visit **eCommerceMasterPlan.com** for more information and case studies of businesses with different eCommerce Business Structures, PRSs and USPs.

What Sort of eCommerce Business Are You?
- Identify your eCommerce Business Structure
- Identify the Scale of Your Product Range
- Differentiate your Business

Establishing The Core Foundations
- Build the Right Website
- Build your Business for Profit and Growth
- Select your Products and Promotions

I Have Built It: Why haven't they come? (aka Marketing!)
- Research your Marketing Plan
- Creating your Marketing Plan
- Test, Measure and Optimise your Marketing

Identifying your eCommerce Business Structure, Product Range Scale (PRS) and Unique Selling Point (USP) has shown you what sort of eCommerce business you are going to build.

Now we can start building the three Core Foundations of your eCommerce MasterPlan:

- **Core Foundation 1: Building the right website.**
- **Core Foundation 2: Building your business for profit and growth.**
- **Core Foundation 3: Selecting your products and promotions.**

To have a sustainable and successful business, you need to get these three right. If they're not right, then everything else you do won't work so well, for example your marketing will be ineffective:

- The wrong website won't convert the traffic into sales.
- If there's not enough margin in your products, you won't be able to afford enough marketing to build the business.
- If you've not got the right products, you won't sell anything, and if the promotions aren't right, you'll be giving away the wrong thing!

Not only that, but these three Core Foundations are pretty hard to change (by hard, I mean expensive, time consuming and slow!) so it's really worth approaching each one in the right way the first time!

WORKBOOK
You can download the workbook for Step 2 or each individual chapter at **eCommerceMasterPlan.com/Free**

CHAPTER 4

Building the Right Website

The website is the most important part of any eCommerce business. What sort of website do you need? How do you build it quickly and effectively? How do you find the right PiggyBack website? Plus, how can you avoid conversion blockers?

The website is the first of the three Core Foundations of the eCommerce MasterPlan that we're going to tackle. The website is also the hardest of the three Core Foundations to fix if it goes wrong, and has no intrinsic value.

eCommerce is all about selling products online. Your website is responsible for displaying your products, getting the visitors to add those products to the basket, and also making sure they order. If your website doesn't do its job, everything else in your business will be more difficult. Even if you have got the best products and marketing in the world, you are not going to sell very much if your website isn't pulling its weight.

For two of the eCommerce Business Structures, it's not a case of building a website, rather choosing a website to represent them. But choosing the website is still critical for the PiggyBackers, and over the lifetime of the business they may well end up building a site at some point. There are sections in this Step that deal purely with the needs of the PiggyBackers and the non-PiggyBackers, but I would recommend you read all sections at some point, as they contain information useful to every eCommerce business.

We're going to look at:

- the role of the website
- how to get your site build right first time
- selecting the right PiggyBack website
- your website's most important job – conversions

. . . .

What Does the Website Need to Do?

An eCommerce website is hard to get right because it has to do so many things, and the list increases all the time:

- Showcase your products.
- Create/represent your brand. (For those transacting online only, this is the only place where your brand exists.)
- Support your marketing activity.
- Convert well – that is, get people to buy.
- Capture customer information.
- Deliver great customer service.
- Meet the legal criteria for selling online.

It's a real juggling act to get this right. Building and getting a site live usually takes at least three months, sometimes over a year, and the costs can be huge – including what you must pay for the site, the impact that not having it has on sales, and the time it takes you to manage the project (time is money, after all).

In the month before writing this chapter, I have spoken to five different businesses (not all eCommerce) that are currently battling to get the site they want. All still have a live website that they first started trying to replace 12 months ago, and all are on at least their second website builder. By taking on the advice in the rest of this chapter, you should be able to avoid such a scenario.

. . . .

Lessons in Site Building

Since 2004, I have been involved in project managing over 20 website builds and redesigns on over 10 different software platforms. Budgets ranged from £2,000 to £150,000, dealing with stakeholders who knew exactly what they wanted and those who didn't; not all the projects went smoothly or ended well. I've learnt a lot.

There are some things that are common across every project I have been involved in, or heard about, and before we go through how to get the website right first time I'm going to run through what you can expect from a successful build process (yes, all of this will be present in the perfect site build).

You Will Fall Out

At some point in the project, you will fall out with your website builder.

It might not be a screaming match, but during the build or sign-off phase there will be a point at which you seriously consider sacking the website builders.

It's natural. It's a massive project, it's really complex, you have a massive amount invested in the process, and it's a scary process. It's a process that will take months, and it's not until the site gets delivered that you find out if it was worth it. Of course you are going to fall out with them, or be disappointed. If the whole thing goes smoothly, 100% of the way through, then you have not pushed hard enough to get the site you want.

The Last Week Before the Site Goes Live Will be Crazy

There will be so much to do – so many pages to proof, so much content to upload and check, endless testing of checkout functionality. You will wonder what you did before the website build project started.

You will underestimate the time required to do all the testing, and a world of little issues will crop up.

When the Site Finally Goes Live, You'll Want to Hug/Send a Bottle of Champagne to Your Site Builders

Until a website is finished and live, it's hard to see how it's really going to work because the only true measure is what it does to your sales (one of the reasons you will fall out). In the last few days, it will suddenly come together and, once the site is live, you'll finally realise the benefits the site has brought you – sales will go up, the stock will finally be integrated, you won't be printing off orders any more. At this point, you will be just a little bit in love with your website builder and very, very relieved.

Other Issues

During site builds you'll also come across these common issues:

- Timescales will stretch and there will be nothing you can do about it (never announce the live date to the press until the day after it happens).
- Something that's not in the brief will become critical to your business: you need a video, Google's changed its algorithm, you have bought a range of products with a different sizing structure.

 Top Tip

I strongly advise anyone who's about to build a website, or has just finished one (actually anyone in eCommerce) to read *Boo Hoo* by Ernst Malmsten. It's the story of boo.com from inception to crash, just 18 months in which they burnt through $135 million. Although all of it happened in 2000, so many of the tales in the book will make anyone involved in a website build giggle and/or roll their eyes.

On the website **eCommerceMasterPlan.com** you'll find a list of really useful books for eCommerce people including a link to *Boo Hoo*.

How to Get Your Site Build Right First Time

WORKBOOK
You can download various useful tools for planning and managing a website build from **eCommerceMasterPlan. com/Free**. Including a workbook for this section.

Hopefully, I haven't scared you off the idea of building an eCommerce website.

The key to a successful build lies in the planning. This is also the key to getting value for money yet having the functionality you need. Most builds that fail do so because either:

- the in-house stakeholders aren't in agreement, so the scope changes
- the brief wasn't detailed enough
- what the merchant wrote in the brief and what the website builder read in the brief was understood in different ways: you said 'Zoom' and meant bigger-picture-in-a-pop-up; they heard 'Zoom' and thought interactive zoom in the style of Google Maps.

The majority of the failures are built in at the start of the project. That's great because it means you can easily build them out of the project.

To do that you need a great brief, but before you can write the brief you need to identify and talk to your stakeholders. We're going to go through each step below, and I strongly advise you to follow this process whether you're creating a totally new site or just refreshing your existing site.

1 Stakeholders

These are the people around the business (or, if a small organisation, the different hats you yourself wear) who have different needs from the website. As a minimum, this should include:

- The product team (buyers and merchandising) – get them involved so you know what the products are and how you need to sell them. Do the products have different sizing or colours? What information needs to be displayed with each product?
- Online merchandisers – what do they need to be able to do with the content management system (CMS)?
- Customer services – find out what key problems the customers have; how can the new site fix these? (FAQs, 'how to build it' videos, 'call us/email us' buttons.)
- IT/warehouse – integration. It's critical to get this right as it can save hours and money. Find out what integration they need, and how best to do it.
- Finance – what payment methods are you using/can you use?
- Marketing – what feeds and tracking do they need? What is required for search engine optimisation (SEO), for social media? What promotions does the website need to be able to run?
- Brand – what should the site look like?
- The owner.

In your business there may be more stakeholders than this, so take half an hour to consider who needs to be involved and why. Then work out the easiest way to do this – a half-day meeting? An email questionnaire?

Make sure you also future-proof the site. It's not just about what you need today; discussions should include what's going to be needed over the next 12–36 months. If you're about to launch a range of personalised items, you need the website to be ready.

There are a lot of areas of input into a website for an eCommerce business; it's important to get them all understood early in the process because it will make the whole project easier to manage AND make sure you get the right site.

Once you have the input of all the stakeholders, you may find conflict between them about what they all want. You will have to resolve these conflicts before putting the site out to tender.

2 The Brief

The brief is the document you are going to send out to the companies who are going to tender for the job of building your website. The brief enables you to make sure everything your company needs is going to be provided.

Make the brief really detailed; if it's less than five pages, it does not contain enough information. You may want to include mock-ups of how it might look, as well as an example set of product data. The more detail you put in, the more effective the tendering process will be, and the smoother the website build project.

Once you are happy with the brief, get each stakeholder to check it over: if you get them to all agree at this point, it makes the rest of the process much more straightforward. Also explain to them what their involvement from here on in will be. You need to manage their expectations and their involvement – what will you need them to sign off at the end of the project, if anything?

As well as all the detailed information, it is worth putting in some background colour to the project: why do you want the new site? What are your hopes for it? Plus an estimate of site traffic volumes – hosting is expensive and a slow site will kill your sales.

Be aware, however, that the brief will change between you sending it to the website builders and when you sign on the dotted line and the project actually kicks off. That's because your website builders will have ideas about how the site in your brief can be improved further; things you thought would be out of the price range may not be, and it may be possible to do other things better. Finally, there may be one item you have included that's not critical and adds substantially to either timescales or cost. You need to feed these changes back to your stakeholders to make sure everyone's happy.

Top Tip
Often overlooked points to put in your website brief:

(Some of these add clarity to what you would normally put; others are little extras it's worth getting added in.)

- Google Shopping Feed.
- Postcode Anywhere Integration (for postal address entering).
- Google Webmaster Tools, including XML Feeds.
- 301 redirect (if it's not your first website).
- Mobile responsive design.
- Multiple checkout – Amazon? PayPal?
- RSS feed for the blog.
- Full Google Analytics tracking – including search and eCommerce.
- A checkout with conversion funnel reporting.
- URL structure for SEO.
- Auto-generating metadata for SEO.
- Outline all the promotions you are going to want to run.
- Outline how you will categorise your products, and the data you have to display for them.
- Include which browser/operating system configurations you want the site to work on. (There is a list of the current ones to include on the website **eCommerceMasterPlan.com/Free.**)

3 The Tender Process

Once the whole company is happy with the brief, it can be sent to the website builders. If you are running a full tender process, then pick three to five different builders, but make sure each would be able to do the job for you; an initial exploratory phone call can save everyone a lot of time.

Each builder will come back to you in a different way. That's OK. The structure they come back with enables them to fit their technology to your needs in the easiest way for them. You want them to do a good job if you pick them, so making it easy for them to do the job will save you time, money and reduce errors. Letting them respond in their own style also gives you an insight into how they work, and that's a great thing to find out, too.

From each builder you will expect to get back:

- Pricing – both build cost and future maintenance costs such as hosting fees. Ideally, the cost will be broken down so you can see if you want to exclude anything. Never only buy a website based on the build price. Website pricing is more complicated than that. There will always be follow-on costs, hosting, software license fees, maintenance and support retainers. You need to factor in what these are, and fully understand what is and isn't covered in the overall price. Try to extrapolate each builder's fees over 12–24 months to get a proper basis for comparison.
- Timescales – these might be exact dates, or simply usual timeframes.
- References – a few customers you can speak to.

In addition to what the builders send back, you are going to want to meet with them. Each meeting you have will prompt fresh questions, so I'd recommend meeting the 'worst' first and your favourite last. There are a few critical things to include in the meeting:

- Question anything that doesn't make sense to you in their response. This is your opportunity to really understand what they can/can't do for you.
- Have a live run-through of their back end system – you want to understand how easy the CMS (Content Management System) is to use, and how much functionality it gives you. Explore everything: this is often the stage at which you find out a few bits that don't meet your expectation.
- Explore the front end (what the customer sees). How much can you change? What is totally set in stone?
- You might also want them to provide some mocked-up artwork to prove they understand your brand.
- Ask about timescales: when can they fit in your build? How busy are they right now?
- Don't forget to make sure your systems team is happy with the integration plans.
- How much stretch have the builders allowed for in the project? What happens if the costs and timescales grow beyond this?

It will be a long meeting...

Once you have had the meeting and you have got their prices, you need to speak to people whom they have already built sites for and road-test their websites. Key questions to ask previous clients are:

- Was the project on time?
- Was the project on budget?
- How were they to work with?
- How have the support and costs been since the site went live?

The last question is possibly the most important. If the site build goes well, you could be working with the company for years. You need to understand what they are like to work with post-live.

4 Signing and Kicking Off

Once you are happy you have found the right website builder, you are going to need to sign some sort of contract with them. This is a great opportunity to finalise exactly what's in the brief. It won't be the same one that you sent to them in the beginning; you'll have learnt things you want to include during the tender process, and they will have pulled the brief into their format. So, before you sign, take time to make sure all of you are 100% agreed on the final scope, pricing, payment plan and timescales.

5 The Build

You quickly need to get clarity on the detail in the timescales/project plan. What do you need to supply? When is everything required? When are members of your team going to need to be ready to sign off? And how much movement is there in the plan?

Put all the important dates in your diary – and in the diary of anyone else who needs to contribute.

Keep referring back to the agreed scope. Try not to go beyond it and, if the builders are not following it, bring them back on track as soon as possible.

Most website builders will tell you they have a project manager who will oversee everything for you. I have never worked with one who successfully does. I have worked with many great website-builder-side project managers, but, however good they are, they are not a member of your team; they are a member of the website builder's team. They don't understand what you are trying to achieve as well as you do, and they are highly unlikely to invest time motivating your team to provide things on time and correctly. So you need to manage the project, too.

As soon as you are underway, convert the brief/to do list into whatever format you need it to be in to make sure everything happens and happens right. The format should be what works for you – be that a mind map, a project planning tool, an Excel spreadsheet, a Google doc or a very large whiteboard. Get everything on it and explain to the key people how it's to be used (especially the website-builder-side project manager). If you do it really successfully, it will become your key method of communication with the website builders – the foundation of every call and meeting agenda.

DOWNLOAD...
There's an example website project planner available on the website at **eCommerceMasterPlan.com/Free**

6 Putting the New Site Live

The first rule of putting the new website live is to make sure you are 100% happy with it. Test everything again and again and again. For most website builders, the point when the website goes live marks the end of the build phase – so usually any changes after that are chargeable.

It is always tempting to go live with a few things outstanding in order to hit the deadline, but be very careful if you do because you might be stuck with a very large bill.

A few days before the site goes live, make sure you have got access to the DNS hosting for your domain (www.yourwebsite.com). Then change the TTL to a few minutes or seconds; the TTL is the Time to Live – that is how often your domain records are refreshed so, if it's set to 24 hours, it will take a long time for your new website to go live.

Once you're ready to go live:

- turn off all your marketing activity
- tell customer services
- at the appointed time change the A record to point to the new hosting IP address

Once you have changed the A record, there are a few things you need to do almost immediately.

The first is to check the site is working. Place a few orders, do some navigating, sign up for emails, etc. Make sure it's all working on the front end, but also that any data submitted is ending up where it should (orders to the warehouse, email sign-ups to your database, etc.).

Once you are happy, let the rest of the business know it's changed over. Be ready to deal with 'but I can still see the old site', and have IT refresh the office cache and individuals' PC caches. It is probably best to explain to everyone that DNS propagation can take a while as all the name-servers around the internet are updated with your new hosting location; this can take a couple of days. An annoying headache, but it is always either the most PC-incompetent person in the office or the boss whose computer is the last to see the new website.

Next, you need to check and set up the non-critical functionality of the new website (that's the stuff that the customers won't have noticed). Is all your tracking code working – analytics and reporting, etc? At this point, you also want to make sure Google Shopping, Webmaster Tools, etc. are picking up on new feeds.

Once all this is done you can turn the marketing back on.

Finally, monitor the performance and tweak what you need to; a website is never finished.

· ·

Selecting the Right PiggyBack Site

Unlike getting the build of your own website wrong, it's not that financially expensive if you get the choice of a PiggyBack website wrong, although you will still lose all the time you have spent getting your account set up, your shop sorted out and your products listed – so it's worth trying to make the right decision first time.

The other big difference is that you can use multiple PiggyBack sites; you are not restricted to just the one website.

WORKBOOK
You can download a workbook for this section from
eCommerceMasterPlan.com/Free

How to Choose Your PiggyBack Websites

The decision will be based on three areas:

1 Financial – how much does it cost you to put your products on the website? What is the model of charges? This varies from a monthly subscription to a simple commission – and everything in between.

2 Systems – can you integrate with your own systems? How easy is it to upload products? How easy is it to process orders and deal with queries? How helpful and accessible are the PiggyBack sites when you need them?

3 Marketing – what's the PiggyBack site's customer base? How well do they market you? What help do they provide? How easy is it to customise your 'shop'?

The importance of these three areas will depend on your needs and the strategy of your business. If you are a designer selling a few really attractive products, then 'shop' customisation and how the products look is going to be more important than pricing or systems. If you are selling in your spare time and don't like technology very much, then systems and the fees structure is going to be really key; you don't want to be paying a subscription in months when you have nothing for sale. If you are interested in selling lots of products, systems and marketing are going to be key.

The very first thing you need to do is find out what options there are in your marketplace. You can do this by simply searching on Google for products like yours and seeing where they are being sold. It's also a good idea to tap into some industry knowledge: get on the forums frequented by businesses selling similar products and find out where they sell.

Once you have got the list, start by simply looking at each of the sites and ask yourself if it's somewhere you would be happy for your products to be promoted. If it's not, take it off the list. Although this is rather subjective, it's important to be on websites that enhance your brand, and where people would expect to find your products.

PiggyBack Site Selection Checklist

Next, you need to work through the following checklist so that you can compare your options. The checklist is split into three areas: Financial Criteria, Systems Criteria and Marketing Criteria.

DOWNLOAD...
On the website (at **eCommerceMasterPlan.com/Free**) we have created a directory of PiggyBack websites, so have a look to see what's in your marketplace.

Financial Criteria

- Is there a set-up cost? What is it?
- Is there a subscription fee (a fee you must pay every year/month/day whether or not you sell anything)? How much is it?
- Are there listing fees (a fee for each item you list)? How much?
- Is there a commission on your sales? How much?
- How does postage charging work?
- What's the payment method? Do they take the money and pass it on to you, or do you need to take the money yourself – through a PayPal account, for example?
- How do you get paid? How soon do you get the money? If you are using your own PayPal account, it will be almost instant, but if they are taking the money, how long will it be before you get paid?

Once you have the answers to all these questions you will need to model what the charges on each are going to add up to for your business. So estimate a month's sales and calculate how much it's going to cost you in fees. Don't forget to work out how much postage will cost. Then you have got a price per month that allows you to compare the sites.

Systems Criteria

The systems criteria checklist will be different for each business, so if one of these is irrelevant to you, leave it out. This set of criteria isn't as easy to compare as the financial criteria, so give each website a mark out of five in each area for how well they meet what you need, and then total them up.

- Can you integrate with your own systems? If you have an existing product system or order-taking system, can you integrate it all? How easy is it? How much will it cost?
- How easy is it to upload products? Can you use a spreadsheet to bulk upload, or does each need to be done separately?
- How many images can you upload for each item?
- Can you upload video or audio for the products?
- How easy is it to process orders and deal with queries? Do they have a communication centre you can use for this, or do you have to manage it via your own email account?
- How helpful and accessible are the PiggyBack sites when you need them? Do you get a phone number to call, or is it just a help centre?

Marketing Criteria

Again, give each website a mark out of five in each area for how well they meet what you need, and then total them up.

- Who is the customer base? Does it fit with your target customers?

- How busy is their site? You really want a number of visitors, rather than hits or page views.
- How much do their customers buy? What's the conversion rate? Average Order Value (AOV)?
- In what ways will the site promote you? Emails? Search advertising? Features on the website or blog?
- Can you customise your 'shop'?
- What help do they give you to increase your sales? Webinars, training, advice? (Etsy is great at this.)
- How well SEO-ed will your product pages be? Can you affect this?
- Do they have social sharing buttons on the product pages?
- Do they have a customer review or comments system?
- Do they feed into Google Shopping?
- Is there an option to buy extra promotion on the site? How much is it?
- How good is their on-site search engine? Try a few searches and see if you get relevant results.
- Can you cross-sell your products?
- What promotions can you run?

Some of these marketing elements might not seem immediately important right now, but if you've read my book *eCommerce Marketing* you'll see why you need to get a head start.

Once all the data is gathered, it should be easy to whittle down your list to the top two or three you are going to try out. Don't start them all at once. Pick the best option and start building that first: get your account set up, get your shop ready, set up your products, and deal with at least a few weeks' worth of orders – making changes as you go. Once you are happy that you have got that site working well for you, then – and only then – move on to site number two. If you try to do all of them at once, you risk getting confused and it may take forever to get each one working for you. Plus, you'll learn lots with each launch that you can use to make the next one easier and better.

As you use the PiggyBack sites, you'll find that different products work well on different sites – so focus your efforts on those. You may find one site doesn't work for you, or stops working for you; don't be afraid to pull out, or at least cut back the product range you have there.

Why Use More than One PiggyBack Website?

If you are a mainstream PiggyBacker, then you are pretty much limited to two websites: Amazon and eBay (although there are new options coming along all the time – Play.com, Tesco, and more). You will most likely end up on both Amazon and eBay because that's how you maximise your sales. Both attract a mainstream audience, but there are lots of people who only use one of these, so you will miss out on sales if you don't use them both.

For the Niche PiggyBacker, there are hundreds of choices, and they are often difficult to compare until you have tried them out. Each also taps into a slightly different market; some are international, some are just for one country, so you want to test out one or two to make sure you find the place that will sell your products the fastest and the most profitably.

Put simply, you should use more than one PiggyBack site in order to get your products in front of multiple audiences, increase your sales and spread the risk.

Your Website's Most Important Job

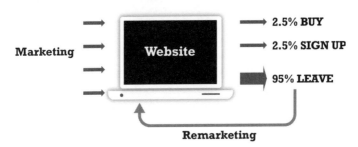

Whatever type of site you need, remember that a good eCommerce website must:

- convert traffic to sales
- represent your brand well
- attract customers.

The most important of these is to convert the traffic to sales. If your website doesn't convert the traffic to sales easily, then everything you do to get people to your website will be slightly wasted.

Consider the simple equation:

$$\left[\text{Traffic}\right] \times \left[\begin{array}{c}\text{Average} \\ \text{Order Value} \\ \text{(AOV)}\end{array}\right] \times \left[\begin{array}{c}\text{Conversion} \\ \text{Rate}\end{array}\right] = \left[\text{Sales}\right]$$

If each month you get 1,000 people to your website and your average order value is £50, consider the impact of a stronger conversation rate:

A POORLY CONVERTING WEBSITE:

Traffic = 1,000
AOV = £50
Conversion Rate = 1.5%

$$\boxed{1,000} \times \boxed{£50} \times \boxed{1.5\%} = \boxed{£750}$$

IF THE WEBSITE CONVERTS JUST A LITTLE BETTER:

Traffic = 1,000
AOV = £50
Conversion Rate = 2.5%

$$\boxed{1,000} \times \boxed{£50} \times \boxed{2.5\%} = \boxed{£1,250}$$

That's a 60% sales increase. It's not difficult to get a website to convert at 2.5%, but many don't. A well put-together website will also help increase your AOV.

. . . .

Tackling Barriers to Conversion

To ensure your website does its job properly, you need to remove as many barriers to conversion as possible.

A barrier to conversion is anything that stops the customer from buying from you. Most are based on confusion, uncertainty or distraction. If a customer is confused, they won't buy. If a customer is uncertain that what you are selling is what they want, they won't buy, and if they get distracted, they'll forget to buy.

The first step is to find those barriers. To do this you need to look at the website stats. Where are people leaving your conversion funnel, where do they exit the site from? What products are most often put in the basket but not bought? Then look at your website, go through it from beginning to end and look out for areas of uncertainty, potential confusion and distractions.

Common Barriers to Conversion

- Navigation in the checkout – take a look at Amazon's checkout; once you are in the basket, there's nothing you can do but proceed with your order.
- Buttons – are your buying buttons easy to follow? Do you always put the one to proceed in the same place and in the same colour? Are the words on the buttons clear and do they promote an action? 'Buy now' will work better than 'Buy'.
- Hidden Postage – make sure your customer is aware of postage options early on, as soon as they get to the website. Lots of people will drop out if they get to the checkout and suddenly get hit with a £5 charge they weren't expecting.
- Delivery Speeds – be upfront about these too. When people buy, they want to know when they are going to receive their order.
- Contact Details – don't hide them. Let people know how to call or email you, and explain how fast you'll get back to them if they do. They may well not call, but if they know they can, then that reduces their uncertainty and increases their trust in you. Your address is important, too.

- Product Information – with the exception of delivery, this is the major cause of confusion and uncertainty. Include the information the customer needs. Sizes, dimensions and some compelling written copy are really key.
- Product Photos – if the dress is available in blue, the customer needs to see the whole dress in blue – not just a swatch of that colour.
- Promotions – make 'em simple. Really simple. If there's anything complex, then keep explaining what the customer needs to do.

Plus, there is one thing you can do to improve conversion across the board, and reduce the impact of customer confusion, uncertainty and distraction: that is to **prove that customers can trust you**. If they trust you and like you, they are going to persist a little more to make that purchase, they are less likely to be confused, and they will trust that the areas they are uncertain about will be OK and, if not, they know you will honour a refund. A customer who trusts you is far more likely to remember to come back post-distraction and make the purchase.

If your chosen USP is Customer Service, then you have pretty much got that wrapped up; likewise if you have a strong brand or strong customer base. Whatever your relationship with your customers, there are a few things you can do to the website to help build that trust:

- Add security logos of the credit cards you accept to the site, whichever service you are using to secure your payment area – Sagepay or Verisign. These increase customer trust.
- Have a proper Privacy Policy and Terms and Conditions – and don't hide them. Writing them so they can be read easily is also helpful.
- Fix anything that's broken.
- Have a clear and easy-to-find and read returns policy.
- Think about adding a guarantee. (As I'm proofing this I've just been distracted by the shoe shop Schuh which has a 12-month returns

policy for unworn shoes – Not sure if they'll go with your dress? Buy 'em and take 'em home – you've got 12 months to get them back to us.)

- Have an 'About Us' page; show who you are. And include your company history.
- Awards help, too, as do the ISIS and IDIS logos managed by the IMRG (see IMRG.org).
- Look at what questions customers regularly ask and write answers to them – FAQs.

Your eCommerce website is at the centre of your business. If it doesn't work, your business will fail. Invest as much time and money as you can into getting it right, but invest wisely. On day one, an eCommerce business can do very well on a site that only costs a few thousand pounds, but if you are a bigger business, your site must live up to customer expectations.

. . . .

Chapter 4 Complete: What's Next?

A website can take a few months to build and be ready to go live and it's not a project you want to rush! So whilst it's being built you can be working on the other two Core Foundations.

- Core Foundation 1: Building your perfect website
- Core Foundation 2: Building your business for profit and growth
- Core Foundation 3: Selecting your products and promotions

NOTES

What are the key points from this section?

_____

_____

_____

_____

_____

_____

_____

_____

_____

_____

_____

_____

WEBSITE

You'll find more ideas for improving conversion and building a better website at **eCommerceMasterPlan.com**

CHAPTER 5

Building Your Business for Profit and Growth

To build the basis for future profit and growth, you need to get a handle on the key numbers in an eCommerce business. That is, the overheads, the margin and the return on investment (ROI). Then you will know what you need to achieve. If you start out in eCommerce without understanding your Overheads, Margin, Cashflow or ROI you are really going to struggle – you'll be walking blind. In Chapter 4, we looked at the key sales equation for an eCommerce business:

$$\left[\text{Traffic} \right] \times \left[\begin{array}{c} \textbf{Average} \\ \textbf{Order Value} \\ \textbf{(AOV)} \end{array} \right] \times \left[\begin{array}{c} \textbf{Conversion} \\ \textbf{Rate} \end{array} \right] = \left[\text{Sales} \right]$$

Unfortunately, eCommerce isn't quite that simple; you can't survive on sales alone. You need to be making a profit. The good news is that a successful eCommerce business can build profit into the model from day one. To do this, you need to understand a few key financial metrics and set them for your business. This includes:

- setting the right margin level for your products (the margin is the difference between what you buy the product for and what you sell it for)

- understanding what your overheads are and how much you need to sell to cover them
- using a return on investment (ROI) calculation to properly analyse the business and make sure you are always maximising your profit through continuous optimisation

Put simply, optimisation is the process of deciding what to keep doing, what to stop doing and what to work harder at.

Before you can dive in to products, promotions and marketing, you need to make sure you have got a firm grip on the financials of your business. That way, you can be certain your efforts will lead to profit.

Many people think that maths and understanding the financials of a business is hard – it's not. Once you've grasped the simple sums below, you'll be able to set the right numbers for your business and then just get on with driving the sales…

It's these 'right numbers' that we're going to identify in this chapter.

WORKBOOK

A workbook to help you identify these ways for making profit for your business can be downloaded from the website **eCommerceMasterPlan.com/Free**

Margin – the Foundation of Your Future Profit

At the heart of any eCommerce success lies a good, sustainable margin.

The margin is the difference between the price you pay for your stock and the amount for which you sell it to your customers. It is quite easy to identify your margin, but it's much harder to work out what it should be – and to keep it there.

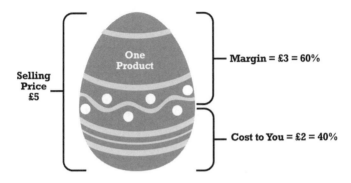

Your Margin is Not Your Profit.

As well as providing your profit, the margin has to cover all your overheads (warehousing, website, staff, power, etc.). Every product you sell needs to contribute to the overhead costs. Once all the bills are paid (the overheads and the product buying), whatever you are left with is your profit.

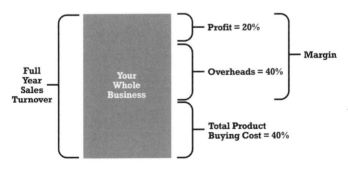

So every product you sell has an impact on how much profit you'll make at the end of the year. That profit is tied up in the margin. So the greater your margin, the more space you have to play with – space for errors, testing, marketing, and more.

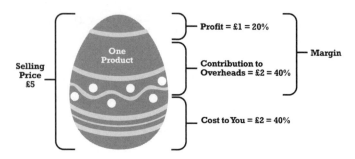

Your maximum margin is set when you buy your stock. So, it's critical to buy every product at the right margin or you won't make any money, or – even worse – you won't be able to cover your overheads.

Aim for a similar margin across all your products (with maybe a 10% tolerance – so it might be 45–55%) and if you can't make your margin on an item, be ready not to stock it.

. . . .

Scale – Covering Your Overheads First (then it's All Profit)

As long as you make your margin on every product you sell, you'll turn a profit – right?

Wrong.

Remember, your margin is covering profit **and** overheads, but the overheads are the same however many products you sell. This means you need to hit a certain value of sales before you start making any profit.

This level is called the 'break even' level.

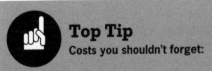

Top Tip
Costs you shouldn't forget:

- Utilities (electric, gas, water).
- Rent and business rates.
- Warehousing.
- Accountants.
- Lawyers.
- Software licenses.
- Salaries and National Insurance.
- Packing materials.
- Stationery.
- Computers.
- Phones.
- IT support.
- Returns and written-off stock.
- Tax – Corporation and VAT.

Your overheads for the year are basically fixed, so you need to generate a certain volume of orders to cover them. For example:

Overheads = £100,000
Margin = 40%
Average Order Value = £50

$$\left[\begin{array}{c}\textbf{Margin} \\ \textbf{Per} \\ \textbf{Order}\end{array}\right] \begin{array}{c}= \\ = \\ =\end{array} \left[\begin{array}{l}\textbf{Average Order Value} \times \textbf{Margin} \\ \textbf{£50} \times \textbf{40\%} \\ \textbf{£20}\end{array}\right]$$

$$\left[\begin{array}{c}\textbf{Orders} \\ \textbf{Required} \\ \textbf{to Cover} \\ \textbf{Overheads}\end{array}\right] \begin{array}{c}= \\ = \\ =\end{array} \left[\begin{array}{l}\textbf{Overhead} \div \textbf{Margin Per Order} \\ \textbf{£100,000} \div \textbf{£20} \\ \textbf{5,000}\end{array}\right]$$

$$\left[\begin{array}{c}\textbf{Sales} \\ \textbf{Value} \\ \textbf{to Cover} \\ \textbf{Overheads}\end{array}\right] \begin{array}{c}= \\ = \\ =\end{array} \left[\begin{array}{l}\textbf{Orders Required to} \times \textbf{Average} \\ \textbf{Cover Overheads} \quad \textbf{Order Value} \\ \textbf{5,000} \times \textbf{£50} \\ \textbf{£250,000}\end{array}\right]$$

In this example, you would need to generate 5,000 orders to break even. It will only be from the 5,001st order that you see a profit (assuming the margin holds and the overheads come in on budget). You can also see here that the sales required to cover the overheads are a LOT higher value than the overheads themselves – that's because of the cost of buying in the products.

From this, you can now work out how many sales you'll need to drive to make the profit you want. If you want a £50,000 profit, then:

Sales Value to Cover Overheads = £250,000
Required Profit   = £ 50,000

$$\begin{bmatrix} \text{Total} \\ \text{Sales for} \\ \text{Required} \\ \text{Profit} \end{bmatrix} = \begin{bmatrix} \text{Sales Value to } + \text{ Required} \\ \text{Cover Overheads } \text{ Profit} \\ \text{£250,000} + \text{£50,000} \\ \text{£300,000} \end{bmatrix}$$

$$\begin{bmatrix} \text{Total} \\ \text{Orders} \\ \text{Required} \end{bmatrix} = \begin{bmatrix} \text{Total Sales } \div \text{ Average} \\ \text{Required } \text{ Order Value} \\ \text{£300,000} \div \text{£50} \\ \text{6,000 Orders} \end{bmatrix}$$

Once you know how many orders you need to drive over the year to achieve the profit you want, break that down into monthly and weekly targets – don't forget to allow for seasonal trends too! Then work to hit those sales volumes.

The impact of a better margin

If we re-run this example with a better margin, then you can quickly see
how improving your margin can make your business easier:

Overheads   = £100,000
Required Profit   = £50,000
Margin   = 50%
Average order value = £50

$$
\begin{bmatrix} \text{Margin} \\ \text{Per} \\ \text{Order} \end{bmatrix} = \begin{bmatrix} \textbf{Average Order Value} \times \textbf{Margin} \\ \text{£50} \times 50\% \\ \text{£25} \end{bmatrix}
$$

$$
\begin{bmatrix} \text{Orders} \\ \text{Required} \\ \text{to Cover} \\ \text{Overheads} \end{bmatrix} = \begin{bmatrix} \textbf{Overhead} \div \textbf{Margin Per Order} \\ \text{£100,000} \div \text{£25} \\ \text{4,000} \end{bmatrix}
$$

$$
\begin{bmatrix} \text{Sales} \\ \text{Value} \\ \text{to Cover} \\ \text{Overheads} \end{bmatrix} = \begin{bmatrix} \textbf{Orders required to} \times \textbf{Average} \\ \textbf{Cover Overheads} \quad \textbf{Order Value} \\ \text{4,000} \times \text{£50} \\ \text{£200,000} \end{bmatrix}
$$

$$
\begin{bmatrix} \text{Total} \\ \text{Sales for} \\ \text{Required} \\ \text{Profit} \end{bmatrix} = \begin{bmatrix} \textbf{Sales Value to} + \textbf{Required} \\ \textbf{Cover Overheads} \quad \textbf{Profit} \\ \text{£200,000} + \text{£50,000} \\ \text{£250,000} \end{bmatrix}
$$

$$
\begin{bmatrix} \text{Total} \\ \text{Orders} \\ \text{Required} \end{bmatrix} = \begin{bmatrix} \textbf{Total Sales} \div \textbf{Average} \\ \textbf{Required} \quad \textbf{Order Value} \\ \text{£250,000} \div \text{£50} \\ \text{5,000 orders} \end{bmatrix}
$$

So just a 10 percentage point improvement in margin means you can
drive 1,000 fewer orders and make the same profit.

ROI – Keeping You On Track

To drive enough sales to hit your profit targets you're going to have to spend some money on marketing and stores, etc. It's very easy to spend all your profit trying to hit your sales targets. To avoid this, as well as keeping an eye on your margin and sales targets, you also need to understand your ROI.

ROI is the number which enables you to see how well you are doing and make decisions on how to do even better. ROI is the profit (Return) on what you have spent (Investment) – it's usually presented as a percentage so you can analyse lots of different types of things against each other:

- Products.
- Product categories.
- Sales channels.
- Marketing methods.
- Seasons.
- Marketing campaigns.
- Weeks or months, year on year.

It doesn't matter if you're comparing a small month to a big month, you'll be able a get a percentage that makes the comparisons really easy.

The formula I use is:

$$\left[\mathbf{ROI}\right] = \left[(\text{sales} - \text{costs}) \div \text{cost}\right]$$

This ROI enables you to compare performance – this year *vs* last year, this month *vs* last month, and see how well your business is doing. It's a quick and easy way to check all is on track and performing well. You're going to be using it to compare like with like – shop *vs* shop, product *vs* product, marketing campaign *vs* marketing campaign.

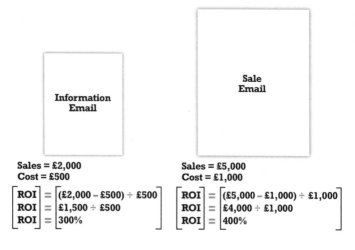

Sales = £2,000
Cost = £500

$$\begin{bmatrix} \text{ROI} \\ \text{ROI} \\ \text{ROI} \end{bmatrix} = \begin{bmatrix} (£2,000 - £500) \div £500 \\ £1,500 \div £500 \\ 300\% \end{bmatrix}$$

Sales = £5,000
Cost = £1,000

$$\begin{bmatrix} \text{ROI} \\ \text{ROI} \\ \text{ROI} \end{bmatrix} = \begin{bmatrix} (£5,000 - £1,000) \div £1,000 \\ £4,000 \div £1,000 \\ 400\% \end{bmatrix}$$

So you don't need to worry about any costs other than those directly attributable to those items. For example:

- When comparing two Google Adwords campaigns, cost = the cost of the clicks.
- When comparing two shops, cost = the cost of running those shops.

To make sure you can quickly use ROI to assess performance, set a simple working ROI like this one:

$$\begin{bmatrix} \textbf{Marketing} \\ \textbf{ROI} \end{bmatrix} = \begin{bmatrix} \textbf{(Sales - Marketing Cost)} \div \textbf{Marketing Cost} \end{bmatrix}$$

This gives you a rough ROI, which ignores product costs and overheads but will enable you to easily measure what's working best. So let's take an example:

CHANNEL	ORDERS	SALES	COST
Email	100	£5,000	£2,000
PPC	60	£2,400	£2,000
eBay	150	£4,500	£500

Taking these numbers, our email ROI will be:

$$\begin{bmatrix} \text{Email} \\ \text{ROI} \end{bmatrix} = \begin{bmatrix} \text{(Sales} - \text{Marketing Cost)} \div \text{Marketing Cost} \\ (£5{,}000 - £2{,}000) \div £2{,}000 \\ 150\% \end{bmatrix}$$

Using the same method, we can work out the ROI for the other channels, too:

CHANNEL	ORDERS	SALES	COST	ROI
Email	100	£5,000	£2,000	150%
PPC	60	£2,400	£2,000	20%
eBay	150	£4,500	£500	800%

From these results we can now see that even though email drives the most sales, the eBay channel is the most profitable.

Alternatively, if you don't like percentages, you can use a profit per order metric:

$$\begin{bmatrix} \textbf{Profit} \\ \textbf{Per} \\ \textbf{Order} \end{bmatrix} = \begin{bmatrix} \textbf{(Sales} - \textbf{Marketing Cost)} \div \textbf{Number of Orders} \end{bmatrix}$$

So, this example would give us:

$$\begin{bmatrix} \textbf{Email} \\ \textbf{Profit} \\ \textbf{Per} \\ \textbf{Order} \end{bmatrix} = \begin{bmatrix} \textbf{(£5,000} - \textbf{£2,000)} \div \textbf{100} \\ \textbf{£3,000} \div \textbf{100} \\ \textbf{£30 Profit Per Order} \end{bmatrix}$$

CHANNEL	ORDERS	SALES	COST	ROI	PROFIT PER ORDER
Email	100	£5,000	£2,000	150%	£30.00
PPC	60	£2,400	£2,000	20%	£6.66
eBay	150	£4,500	£500	800%	£26.66

As you can see above, it's quite useful to work out this metric as well as ROI because here we can see that our email customers are worth more to us than our eBay customers.

So, if you know you can afford to spend £20 on recruiting a new customer, and your marketing channels show a profit per order of £15, then everything is on track. You can use the same theory to look at the ROI of different products, different promotions or even different time periods.

Top Tip
P&P – profit or cost?

As late as the 2000s, the mail order industry aimed to make a healthy profit on its postage and packing (P&P) charges. So, if the customer paid £4.99, the average cost to the merchant was most likely £4, £3 or even less.

Now, it's hard to find a website that doesn't have free P&P over some level of spend – and the level of spend is getting lower year on year. This has been driven by two factors:

- Customers react really positively to free P&P promotions, because a P&P charge is a big blocker to conversion. So why not always have a free P&P offer?
- Businesses whose USP is Customer Service, Delivery and Returns or Customer Base all have good reason to keep the P&P low.

We have seen Amazon taking their minimum free delivery spend ever lower, and also introducing the concept of a subscription delivery service with Amazon Prime. This is being copied by other eCommerce sites: Ocado have a range of different subscriptions depending on whether you want peak-time or off-peak delivery slots.

At the extreme end is Ironmongery Direct (Customer Service USP), who will deliver a £45 order for free on a next day service (so long as you order by 7.30pm). However, they are something of an exception, as most companies only offer free delivery on the cheapest delivery service (usually Royal Mail Second Class) and charge market rates for faster services.

You need to decide what your P&P structure is going to be. Making the wrong decision on your P&P charges can be expensive. So be careful to balance customer service with your own profitability.

Setting Your eCommerce MasterPlan Objectives

In eCommerce, we are bombarded with metrics. It's numbers, numbers, numbers – everywhere. The challenge is often to work out which numbers to focus on. The ones we focus on we call our Key Performance Indicators (KPIs). By identifying your KPIs and using the tools we've run through, you have taken a big step in the right direction.

At the beginning of this section, we looked at the basic business objectives:

- Building profit into your products – your target margin.
- The number of orders you need to cover the overheads: the scale.
- Your target ROI (or profit per order).

None of these is going to be your only objective for the next 12 months.

The analysis you have done so far will have given you some pointers into what your objectives for the year might be, but here are some further commonly-used objectives for eCommerce businesses:

- Average Order Value (AOV) – a great way to increase profitability because you are going to cover more overhead costs with each order, but going for a high AOV can reduce response.
- Conversion Rate – increasing customer response from your marketing is a great way to increase turnover. The more orders you get from each £100 of marketing spend the better!
- Traffic Volumes – if you know your website converts well, then focusing on the traffic you can get to the website makes a lot of sense.
- Sales Value – every company should have sales targets!

- Number of Orders – if you need to acquire customers in the next 12 months, then this is worth focusing on.
- Conversion to Website Buyer – how many of your customers can you get to order online rather than via other channels? If customers ordering online is best for your business (cheaper, etc.), then this can be a useful objective.

It will lead to confusion and you missing targets if you try to aim for all of these objectives, so you need to choose two or three to be your KPIs for the year – the ones you check at least monthly. And there should be at least one KPI for scale and one for ROI (profitability).

WEBSITE
There's lots more on the KPIs for each marketing channel in my book *eCommerce Marketing*, available now at
eCommerceMasterPlan.com

· ·

Chapter 5 Complete: What's Next?

This is probably the most difficult step to work through in your eCommerce MasterPlan – so well done for getting to the end of the chapter!

We've now run through the numbers behind successful eCommerce and how to measure your performance in order to keep your plan on target.

To build your successful eCommerce MasterPlan then, you need to understand:

- your margin
- what profit you want to make
- how many orders you need to generate over the year
- how to use ROI to measure and optimise performance
- which KPIs you will focus on

The next Core Foundation we need to look at is how to use products and promotions to keep the money rolling in.

- Core Foundation 1: Building your perfect website.
- Core Foundation 2: Building your business for profit and growth.
- Core Foundation 3: Selecting your products and promotions.

NOTES

What are the key points from this section?

_____

_____

_____

_____

My margin is:

_____

_____

_____

My desired profit is:

_____

_____

The orders and sales I need to achieve the above are:

_____
_____
_____

My ROI calculation is:

_____
_____
_____

My marketing (or working) ROI calculation is:

_____
_____
_____

My KPIs to focus on are:

_____
_____
_____

Other notes:

_____
_____
_____

WEBSITE
Visit **eCommerceMasterPlan.com** for more information.

CHAPTER 6

Select Your Products and Promotions

Once you know the numbers, you can start organising what your products are going to be, and promotions sit very closely with your product decisions. How many products do you need? What promotions are you going to run? What mix do you need?

Problems with your marketing plan are fairly easy to fix; if one thing isn't working, it can be changed in a day or less, and there are always lots of alternatives to try. Problems with your products and promotions are much harder to fix because it costs more and takes longer to fix. Lead times for product supply are often long, and product is the place where all your cash will get tied up. Many eCommerce businesses close down every year due to cashflow problems because too much of their money has been tied up in stock that wasn't selling fast enough, or driving enough of a margin.

However, products do at least have some sort of cash value; you are normally going to be able to recover some money from the products that aren't working. Your promotions can be changed in a matter of minutes, so if things aren't working, it is easy to change the promotions to make sure the sales are coming in – but don't forget that the wrong promotion is expensive.

If you want your business to succeed, it's worth making sure that you get your products and promotions right and that they work hand in hand to keep your warehouse emptying and the sales coming in. That is exactly what we are going to cover in this chapter.

. . . .

Why Are Products So Important?

In Chapter 5, we looked at the margin and making a profit. The margin you make and the profit you make is created by your products; created by the difference between how much you buy your products for and how much you sell them for; created by having the particular products your customers want to buy in stock, when they want to buy them.

For most eCommerce businesses, the products are the only pieces of the business that actually physically exist: they are the substance of your business. You can get everything else right – customer service, marketing, fulfilment and price – but if the product isn't right, you will not have any sales or customers.

As we saw in Chapter 2, your PRS forms a critical part of your business strategy.

Niche **Department Store**

In many ways, the products you sell are your business – your brand. So, it's really important to get them right. They are also the pulsing financial heart of your success; so not only do they need to be the right products, the numbers need to stack up too.

Don't Ever Think You Can Tick Products Off the To-do List

Like marketing, your products need constant optimisation. You need to monitor the sales and tweak the product mix, pricing and promotion to keep the money rolling in and the warehouse emptying and, ultimately, the cash flowing.

Plus, you will have suppliers changing their prices and service levels: no stock, too much stock, broken stock. The day before getting this section ready for the book I was chatting to a client about the first delivery of stock received from a new supplier – the first three boxes they opened were all damaged – nightmare!

Optimisation is harder and more critical in products than in marketing, because more of what happens is outside of your control. A company I worked for had found the killer product for the summer season: an Indian-style parasol for the garden. It looked stunning. The photography was great and the pricing and the margin were great, so it was decided to make it the main marketing image for the season. Out went the marketing, in came the orders. All was going really well. But, then, a few were sent back. It turned out that there was a fundamental problem and the whole supply had to be recalled. All the existing orders were cancelled, all the customers who already had the product had to send it back and we had to tell all further buyers (the catalogue was still landing!) that they couldn't have it. It was an unforeseeable nightmare that affected the whole business – from customer service and the warehouse right through to finance and marketing. However, it was a company with a very good Buying and Merchandising team, who knew that success wasn't based on one product, it was based on getting the mix right across the range, so the impact of the problem was considerably less than it could have been.

What Does this Product Mix Look Like?

WORKBOOK
Download our product mix plan workbook at
eCommerceMasterPlan.com/Free

A product mix is a bit like customer segmentation; it includes lots of different facets, and getting it right means getting the right balance between each of the areas. In building and optimising the product mix, the following need to be in balance:

- Margin – first and foremost, it is ESSENTIAL to get this right. If your target margin is 60%, then all your products should have a margin close to this.
- Number of suppliers – it saves so much time and effort if you deal with fewer suppliers.
- Product categories – for example, a fashion retailer might know its units need to be split like this:
  - 20% skirts
  - 30% trousers
  - 40% tops
  - 10% coats
- Price points – for example, your products need to fit within certain retail price points:

- 30% under £10
- 10% £10–20
- 10% £20–40
- 40% £40–75
- 10% over £75
- Product range specific – for example, sizing for fashion, colour for fashion or anything that comes in multiple colours, memory size for MP3 players, or manufacturers for phone shops.

Most businesses will also keep 40–70% of the same products from season to season. So analysing the previous season's performance will guide you on how you need to optimise the mix for the next season: slightly fewer under £10, more blue ones…

The mix also needs to make your website and brand appealing to the customer, so you need to be following the trends and knowing what's coming up. In fashion, you need to know what the colours and styles of the coming season are; in hi-tech areas you need to know what is being released in the next season.

Your product mix helps define your brand, so it shouldn't change too radically year on year or you may lose your regular customers.

I Have Got My Product Mix Right, I Know What I Want to Buy: What Next?

Next, you need to work out how much of each item to buy. There is never unlimited money to buy stock, so the products you buy need to be the ones that are going to sell.

Forecasting and Cashflow

Forecasting = working out what you're going to sell, and when – for example, week-by-week sales volumes for each item of stock.

Cashflow = the cash in the bank and how you keep it flowing.

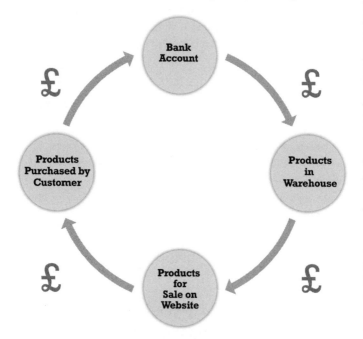

Once you've spent your cash you can't spend it again. So you need to spend the cash on the products based on how quickly they move through the business, whilst taking advantage of bulk-buy discounts.

Any business selling physical goods needs to have an idea of how many of each item it will sell. Even if you are using Drop Ship suppliers (those that hold the stock for you and despatch direct to customers as required), you need to give them an idea of how much of their stock you are going to sell.

It's really important to get the forecasting of sale (by item!) as accurate as possible:

- Your margin may be great, but if you don't have the products, you can't sell them! So you need to make sure you have got stock.
- Backorders are expensive – they use up time and resources, and they annoy customers. So you need to make sure you have got the products in the warehouse before they are ordered by the customer.

You need the right amount of product and you need it now, because until you have got it you can't sell it.

As the title of this section suggests, though, you also don't have unlimited cash and you'll almost always need to pay for the products before the customer pays you for them. Therefore, you need to be really careful about what you buy this month, and what you buy next month.

Your marketing plan will help you work this out; if you are doing a big Valentine's Day promotion, then you need all your hearts, jewellery, chocolates and champagne in the warehouse in January.

Good forecasting will keep your cash flowing and your customers happy!

Two Clear Roles in Getting the Products Right

Put simply, to get your product mix right, you need to do the following:

1   Find products that your customer will like.

2 Make those products stack up into your product mix.

3 Buy the right number of units of each product at the right time.

4 Once the products are on sale, respond to customer demand: not enough demand = discount; too much demand = buy more!

Generally, Part 1 will start up to about a year before the products actually go on sale, and Parts 2 and 3 are happening from about six months before the products are on sale until they are all sold out. The complexity of this means it's usually split into two roles. The Buying team looks after Part 1, the Merchandising team looks after Part 4 – and they collaborate to get Parts 2 and 3 right.

Product selection sits at the core of any eCommerce business because it influences everything else: finance, marketing and the website itself.

Getting the Products Sold – For as Much as Possible, as Quickly as Possible

The faster the products sell, the easier your business is to run. The more the products sell for, the better your margin, the better your business.

Once the products are selected, they need to be promoted and put on the website. There are a few key things that can be done to increase the likelihood of customer purchase, such as the quality of the pictures of the product and the nature of the information about the product.

Remember this?

$$\left[\text{Traffic} \right] \times \left[\begin{array}{c} \textbf{Average} \\ \textbf{Order Value} \\ \text{(AOV)} \end{array} \right] \times \left[\begin{array}{c} \textbf{Conversion} \\ \textbf{Rate} \end{array} \right] = \left[\text{Sales} \right]$$

Well, getting your product information right will help conversions.

The information about your products should be sufficient that all the customers' questions are answered, and that every barrier to purchase is removed.

For example:

- Dimensions – for furniture, the customer needs to know if it will fit in the room; for clothing, the customer needs to know how long the jacket is, how long the trousers are, as well as normal sizing information.
- Add-ons – does it need batteries? If so, what batteries? How many? Are they included? This isn't just for batteries, it's for all sorts of products. If you buy a Dictaphone, does it include a microphone? If buying a Filofax, does it include the contents? Does the holiday include the flights?
- Compatibility – will it work/fit with my existing items? What ports does the TV or laptop have?
- Maintenance – how often do I need to buy the printer cartridges and how much would they cost? When do I need to get the printer serviced?

The questions that need to be answered will differ from product to product. A great way to find out what questions you need to address on the products page is to ask the people who talk to the customers – the call centre operatives, the shop staff – they can tell you what the customers actually want to know. You can find out this information online too – what are customers asking via social media? If you allow reviews of products, what are they saying?

As well as removing barriers to purchase, your product information should sell the product, so you need to write copy that will encourage the purchase.

The pictures can also do a lot to both encourage the sale and remove barriers to it. So make sure your pictures clearly illustrate the product; there are very few products for which just one image will do, as you almost always need the back and front view.

It is very worthwhile adding detailed pictures: the buttons on a cardigan, a picture of the ports on the laptop, everything that comes in the box. The same is true for pictures of the product in action: have a picture of the trousers and a picture of someone wearing them; a picture of the trowel and someone using it.

Photography is not cheap but it's worth investing in. Not only will good photography increase sales, it will also reduce returns of unwanted items because customers are less likely to buy the wrong thing.

The next step is to have videos to illustrate the products. There are very few categories where video isn't going to help. Holiday websites benefit from film clips of the hotels and resorts, toy sellers benefit from showing the toys in action, and the fashion world benefits from mini-catwalk shows.

Some businesses even open this up to customer input. Firebox sells gadgets and modern homeware, and is fanatical about encouraging customers to provide videos and photos of themselves using the products – paying £50 for the really great ones. The company also has fantastically detailed product information.

Cross-sells and Up-sells

As well as increasing conversion rates, cross-sells and up-sells can increase AOV too!

It is possible to have a very long and tedious debate about the difference between cross- and up-sells.

The customer doesn't care what you call them, and whatever you want to call them you need them. You need to make customers aware of alternatives they might want to buy and products that go well with what they're buying/looking at. It might be batteries, handbags that match the shoes, or the right drill bits for that power tool – get it right and sell your products faster!

. . . .

Promotions

WORKBOOK
Get the promotions workbook from the website
eCommerceMasterPlan.com/Free

Whichever of the seven eCommerce Business Structures you are, and whatever your USP, you have to run some form of promotion to grow sales and get your customers to do what you want them to do.

That is the key to promotions – to get your customers to do what you want them to do. Whether that's to buy a certain product, sign up for emails or increase their AOV, it's a promotion that's going to make it happen. Promotions are not necessarily price discounts; for some businesses discounting would damage the brand, so we're talking about all those promotions that can be used to get customers to your site and to buy. This might include:

- free P&P
- free returns
- multibuys
- voucher codes
- sales
- 20% off deals
- free gifts
- half price when you do X
- gift to charity
- prize draw
- the last few available
- brand new
- previews

Promotion Rules

Before we dive into these in more detail, there are a few rules to bear in mind when creating promotions to make sure a promotion works really well.

The first and most important rule is – know what you are trying to make the customer do.

Why you want to run the promotion and what you want the customer to do will change what promotion you put in place. If you need to clear out the rest of the season's stock to generate cash to buy the new season's stock, then a sale with really simple discounting is a great idea. But if you want to increase the AOV, you need to do a multibuy offer or a 'Spend over £X, Save £10'.

Other Rules

1 Margin

Any promotion shouldn't damage your margin. You don't want to do a Hoover[1] and give away something worth more than what the customer has paid. So only run a promotion if you know what it's going to cost you.

2 Easy to Understand

Keep it simple. A promotion should be easy for the customer to grasp or they won't take you up on it.

3 End Date

Urgency is a great way to get people to do something, so promotions should mention an end date. Think 'must end soon', 'only 2 days left', 'only available in June'.

4 Which Channels?

If you are Mail Order, Bricks and Clicks, or Full Multichannel, is the promotion going to run across all your channels or just online?

5 Which Customers?

Do you want to run this offer for everyone or just for your best customers? Or for those who you want to do something in particular? If you are working on upping AOVs, you could have a free gift which one group of customers gets if they spend £50, and another gets if they spend £100.

---

1 The Hoover Free Flights Fiasco happened in 1992. Hoover launched a promotion in the UK giving two free airline tickets to anyone who bought £100 of Hoover products. This proved a very popular promotion, but had two problems: (i) many of the flights cost more than the customer had spent; (ii) it was so popular Hoover ran out of some products. These two combined almost meant the end of Hoover as a business. You can read more about this on Wikipedia, where it has its own page!

6 Spend Barriers

When you have to ship the product to customers, it's always worth thinking about a spend barrier (must spend over Y to qualify). This will help ensure you don't make a loss, and also means the customers who respond are better customers because they want more of your products.

7 Scarcity

Scarcity is a great way to drive a response – 'only 3 available'. Plus, if you're running a giveaway, make sure you limit the number available.

If you think about each of these points before running any promotion, you'll get better results, it will cost you less and you'll avoid running a promotion that damages your business.

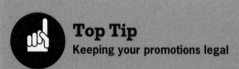

Top Tip
Keeping your promotions legal

There is a lot of legislation about acceptable promotions, and every promotion should have a set of Terms and Conditions somewhere – even if it's just covered in your standard Terms and Conditions. To find the latest legislative guidance, head to **eCommerceMasterPlan.com/Free**.

Key Promotion Types

It would be wrong to write a chapter on promotions without giving you some ideas! So here goes:

Free Delivery

Really powerful: delivery is often a blocker to purchase, so offering it free is a great way to encourage the purchase.

Sale

Generally, you should only have a sale two to four times per year, when you need to clear out the old stock to make way for the new. It makes sense to tie in your sale times with the big boys in your marketplace because they set the customer expectation. A sale should be available to all your customers, but you may want to give a single channel or group of customers an exclusive preview.

Never go to your maximum discount on day one – you want to leave room for marketing further reductions and you don't want to give the margin away if you don't have to!

Category Offers

This is when you take only one product category and discount that: so, '20% off Swimwear' or '25% off Garden Furniture'.

Voucher Codes

To tightly control who can take advantage of an offer, and to track how well an offer is responded to, voucher codes can be really useful. So you could run the same offer for everyone, but give a different code to different customer segments.

Bear in mind that not everyone who responds to the offer will remember to use the voucher, that's fine. Plus, make sure the voucher codes can be used via all sales channels (phone, post, online, etc.).

Multibuys

Multibuys are a great way to encourage customers to get more involved with your brand because it encourages them to spend more. It's also a good way to increase AOV. Be careful with these offers, though, as it can be difficult to make them easy to understand online.

Free Gifts

Free gifts can be a great way to drive sales, but not all free gifts are created equal. A good free gift will be something that:

- fits with your brand
- has an RRP of between £5 and £10
- will appeal to your customers
- could be given as a gift by your customers
- is light and easy to post (to keep your costs down)
- doesn't cost you very much – usually businesses will buy in products specifically as a free gift.

And make sure you have got enough of the free product! There is little worse than wasting lots of customer service time dealing with customers whose free gift is on backorder.

Finally, don't forget to put the free gift item on sale on the website – customers may well want to buy it!

Half Price with Purchase

This is similar to a multibuy and a free gift, but it encourages extra spend/the purchase of another item. So it's one or more products that can be bought at half price when the customer buys something else. Like a free gift, it's worth sourcing these items specifically for the offer.

Prize Draw Entries

This needs to be a compelling prize, but it can be a great way to motivate people to buy.

Gift to Charity

When I worked at Barclays and was trying to get people to sign up to online banking, the best offer we ever ran was a £10 donation to Barnardos for each person who signed up in a month. Charitable donations can be a really great way to encourage customers to buy. Make sure you put a maximum donation in the Terms and Conditions, though.

Last Chance to Buy

A lot of fashion shops are doing this now – a special category on the website where all the end-of-line stock is, still at the original price. This highlights an urgency to buy (a very powerful message) and also tidies up the rest of the website, putting the low-stock items in one place.

Preview/New

A new season launch/preview of a new range is a really compelling opportunity for your best customers.

There are many more ways to encourage customers to buy, and promotions don't have to be about discounts! Do remember to keep a database of current promotions so you can avoid customers using several to get something for free!

Chapter 6 Complete: What's Next?

Getting your products and promotions aligned gives any eCommerce business a great platform for profitable sales and growth and leaves us ready to get on with the marketing.

NOTES

What are the key points from this section?

_____

_____

_____

_____

_____

Other notes:

_____

_____

_____

_____

WEBSITE

Visit **eCommerceMasterPlan.com** for more information on product selection and promotional examples and ideas.

Step 2: Establishing the Core Foundations Complete: What's Next?

. . . .

You should now understand the three Core Foundations of your eCommerce business:

- Core Foundation 1: Build the right website.
- Core Foundation 2: Build your business for profit and growth.
- Core Foundation 3: Select your products and promotions.

Step 2 builds on your understanding of your eCommerce business from Step 1:

- The eCommerce Business Structure – how you get your products in front of your customers.
- The PRS – what you're selling.
- Differentiation – your generic strategy and your USP – what makes your business different.

You should now know what you're selling, how much you need to sell and on what website(s) it will be available. **So now it's time to get cracking with the marketing plan and drive you some traffic!**

NOTES

What are the key points from Step 2?

_____

_____

_____

_____

_____

_____

_____

_____

_____

_____

_____

_____

_____

_____

_____

_____

WEBSITE
Visit **eCommerceMasterPlan.com** for more information and case studies of businesses building the three Core Foundations.

What Sort of eCommerce Business Are You?
- Identify your eCommerce Business Structure
- Identify the Scale of Your Product Range
- Differentiate your Business

Establishing The Core Foundations
- Build the Right Website
- Build your Business for Profit and Growth
- Select your Products and Promotions

I Have Built It: Why haven't they come? (aka Marketing!)
- Research your Marketing Plan
- Creating your Marketing Plan
- Test, Measure and Optimise your Marketing

It's the marketing plan that will bring you your customers and make them spend. Here, we go through how to take the outcomes of the other 2 Steps and build them into a marketing plan.

In Step 1, we identified what sort of eCommerce business you have.

In Step 2, we built the three Core Foundations of your eCommerce business.

We're now ready to use all of this to build the marketing plan that is going to work for you, driving the traffic you need to grow your sales.

....

The Marketing Must Fit With the Website

In Step 2, we talked about the following equation:

$$\left[\text{Traffic}\right] \times \left[\begin{array}{c}\textbf{Average} \\ \textbf{Order Value} \\ \text{(AOV)}\end{array}\right] \times \left[\begin{array}{c}\textbf{Conversion} \\ \textbf{Rate}\end{array}\right] = \left[\text{Sales}\right]$$

If the marketing isn't right, there will be no traffic, which means there is no business. Although much of the marketing can happen without affecting the website, the website has a job to do in attracting traffic as well as just converting it, so some of the marketing does involve changes to the website.

When you rent a physical shop, part of your rent is actually marketing spend. You are buying your position in the place where people go shopping. Your shop's position guarantees you a certain amount of footfall (traffic), and your shop window brings you a certain exposure, allowing you to build some brand awareness.

When you mail a catalogue, or insert one in a newspaper or magazine, you are marketing to the list you have selected, but you are also building an awareness of your brand in people other than those on your list. Catalogues get seen by multiple people, so you are attracting more than just those people already on your list.

Buying a URL (www.), building a website and hosting it somewhere brings you no traffic, no prospective customers. You still need to invest in marketing. For most eCommerce businesses, you will need to invest in offline marketing as well as online marketing if you want to grow fast and attract lots of customers.

Marketing is infinitely changeable, and should be altered frequently as new opportunities present themselves. There are three parts to building your marketing and they form an endless cycle in your business:

- Research – knowing what's going on in and outside your business, and using this to improve it.
- The plan – fail to plan, plan to fail – we all know it, but it is always worth repeating!
- Test, measure, optimise – nothing in marketing is static, it's all changing all the time so you need to be aware of the performance, and keep tweaking and changing that plan to improve performance. Always, always test, test, test.

The Chapters 7–9 will take you through each of these in turn.

WORKBOOK
You can download the workbook for Step 3 or each individual chapter at **eCommerceMasterPlan.com/Free**

CHAPTER 7
Researching Your Marketing Plan

To create a great marketing plan you need to research what should go into it, so before building your marketing plan, you need to undertake research in two areas:

- You need to understand where your business is right now.
- You need to understand what's happening in the marketplace.

Unless you understand both of these, you are going to miss opportunities, fail to avoid pitfalls and create a bad marketing plan.

The first time you do this research it will take a lot of time, but each time after that will be much quicker. It's well worth investing the time to look at everything this first time.

Internal Research

Let's look at what you need to understand about your own business first. For this, you should look back over at least two years (if you have been going that long!). Key questions to answer about your business include the following:

Your Customers

- How many customers do you have? How good are they?
- How frequently do your customers buy? How much do they spend on an average visit?

Customer Behaviour

- How many of your customers order online? And how are they different from your other customers?

Usually, you will find in-store customers spend the least per visit, and catalogue customers the most. But online customers buy the most frequently. What do yours look like? It's particularly key to understand this if you want to migrate customers between channels: what are the opportunities and what are the risks? For example, more sales value, but more orders to process.

Customer Information

- What contact details do you have for your customers, and for how many of them?
- Do you have a working email address for everyone, especially for your best customers? Do you have postal addresses for your enquirers?

Marketing Response

- How do your customers get to your website?
- What's the trigger to them going there? Catalogues, in-store leaflets, search results, emails?

- Which traffic sources drive the most traffic to your website? Which traffic sources drive the best traffic?
- What promotions have you run in the past, and did they perform?

Remember, we want scale and return on investment (ROI) – so by 'best traffic' we mean that it drives lots of orders at a price we can afford.

	SITE VISITS	SALES	ORDERS	AOV	COSTS	ROI
Email	10,000	1,000	50	20	500	100%
PPC	10,000	1,000	50	20	500	100%
Remarketing	10,000	1,000	50	20	500	100%
Search	10,000	1,000	50	20	500	100%
Search - Base	10,000	1,000	50	20	500	100%
Twitter	10,000	1,000	50	20	500	100%
Facebook	10,000	1,000	50	20	500	100%
Pinterest	10,000	1,000	50	20	500	100%

DOWNLOAD...
Grab a free Excel version of this table from the website at
eCommerceMasterPlan.com/Free

All the data for filling in this table should be at your fingertips – most of the figures are from your analytics and management accounts.

Promotion Performance

- Which promotions worked well in the past? Which didn't?

Hard to Measure Marketing

- What other marketing are you currently doing and what impact is it having?

For some marketing activity, it's hard to measure the traffic, and it can take months/years before the traffic impact is felt. So you also need to be looking at how well these are already doing; this might include Facebook Likes, Twitter followers, column inches, mentions in magazines or positions on search engines for your keywords.

Objectives – What the Marketing Plan Will Need to Achieve

In Step 2, we identified your Key Performance Indicators (KPIs) and sales objectives. These are key to understanding what the marketing plan will need to achieve. Gather these into your research.

We need to find out how much more marketing you need to do this year (compared to last year) to achieve those objectives.

Plot last year's performance and your objectives on one graph to easily see where the gap is between the continuity performance and your objectives, plus the level you can't afford to go below.

Filling the gap and making sure you stay ahead of your break-even position is the job of your marketing plan.

You also know the ROI you need to achieve. From this, you can work out how much more you can afford to spend on marketing to make sure you fill the gaps. This, plus the value of last year's marketing spend, is what this year's marketing budget will be.

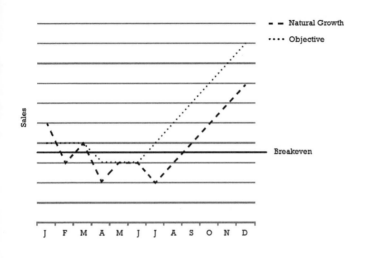

Researching the Marketplace

There are three areas to research and understand in your marketplace:

1 What Are Your Competitors Doing?

What marketing have they been using? What products are they now selling? How have their prices and promotions been over the last year? Go and place some orders with them to see what their process is like. This can give you some ideas of things to test and also things to avoid!

2 What Opportunities and Threats Are There in the Marketplace?

What do you need to be aware of: Royal Mail price increases, big national events, new routes to market, etc?

3 The Marketing Methods at Your Disposal

A mere decade ago, you could test a new marketing list or method one year and, if it worked, roll it out seeing good results for many years. This just isn't the case anymore – you need to roll out marketing methods faster and take advantage of changes and opportunities quickly. This means you need to know what's happening and be ready to react.

What Sort of Marketing Are We Talking About?

There are nine key ways to market/get traffic to your eCommerce website. Not all nine methods are necessary or successful for every business.

WEBSITE
There is lots more on the key KPIs for each marketing channel in my book *eCommerce Marketing*, available now at **eCommerceMasterPlan.com/Books**

1 Content

By content, we mean video, blogs, articles, 'how to' guides, pictures, news, etc. – anything that consumers can consume and share.

We have already touched on content as a way to differentiate your eCommerce business, but it's also a great way to attract customers. Great content will improve your visibility on the search engines, and so bring you lots of traffic. It will also keep customers coming back to you when they need answers, so they will trust you and be more likely to buy from you than from the competition. Content is also key to getting customers to talk about you on social media; it's a great way to gain new customers and increase your traffic from search engines. So content forms the basis of your social media activity too.

2 Email

Email is of no use to you until you have someone to email.

Buying consumer email data is a massive waste of time and money because response rates are very, very low. So you need to use email marketing to keep your customers buying from you. Regular communications to keep customers up to date with your news and promotions are essential for a successful eCommerce business. However, make sure to segment your data to be certain you are sending the right information to the right customers at the right time. It's also useful to make the most of the automatic emails that go out to customers (order confirmations, etc.).

3 Social Media

Social media can bring many benefits to an eCommerce business. It can:

- attract new customers
- build your relationship with existing customers
- encourage repeat purchases
- improve your traffic from search engines
- help with customer service
- build your brand.

However, you shouldn't do it unless you (i) have something to talk to your customers about (just promotional messages are not enough) and (ii) are ready and open for the two-way conversation that will come next. A social media strategy is a big commitment, and it may take many months before it has a measurable impact.

4 Brand Awareness

Unlike a shop or catalogue, a website by itself brings you no brand awareness at all.

So you have to invest in building awareness of your website. This might mean using other marketing methods such as advertising, direct mail, sponsorship or PR. But invest in it you must.

Brand awareness provides a double-whammy benefit. It brings traffic to your website AND it means visitors to your website in general will be more likely to buy because they know you, so they trust you a bit already.

Brand awareness doesn't stop once the first purchase is made, though. You have to live up to your brand, so be aware of your brand impact post purchase. The box the goods arrive in, the packing slip, the whole customer service experience.

5 Offline

Most eCommerce businesses will need to do some offline marketing in order to recruit customers. Offline marketing will frequently give you a quicker, more cost-effective route to a much larger group of core customers than online marketing. This includes:

- trade shows
- catalogue and direct mail
- selling off the page in glossy magazines
- other magazine advertising
- advertorials
- PR.

So don't forget to look away from the screen!

6 Search

Many eCommerce businesses have been built on successfully capturing search traffic. There are some key foundations an eCommerce business needs to put in place to make the most of the search engine opportunity:

- Get the keywords on your website right. If you don't have the right keywords in the right places on your website, you are unlikely to appear in search results.
- Have content.
- If you have a physical location, create your 'place page' – this is a page on Google+ which adds you to location searches.
- Enable people to talk about you online – social sharing is great for search engine optimisation (SEO).

7 Pay Per Click (PPC)

PPC is the fastest way to get quality traffic to your website. You can place ads on Google, Yahoo and Bing that will appear to people searching for your products. You can place ads on Facebook that will appear to people interested in your products. It's really powerful, but it can also be very expensive.

You only pay when someone clicks on your advert, but you'll quickly be running hundreds of adverts. So you need to make sure which of your adverts are working, and which targeting methods (demographic and interests on Facebook, keywords on the search engines) are working. Optimising spend is a complex process, but done right it will bring you some great results.

Don't forget product listing ads on Google – these can be REALLY cost effective.

8 Remarketing

Out of every 100 people who visit your website, fewer than 10 will leave you their details (by ordering or signing up to your social media or email). So 90 people are leaving without a trace.

Remarketing is a way to encourage those 90 people back to your website. So, if someone's been to your site and looked at dresses, you can place ads for your dresses in front of them on other websites. This is a highly-effective way of gaining extra sales and making the most of all your other marketing activity – the activity that got them to your website in the first place.

Remarketing can be run through the Google Adwords system.

9 Partnerships

Partnering with other companies who target the same customer group as you can be hugely effective. There are many ways of doing this, and most are under used by eCommerce businesses.

The oldest method is affiliate marketing: this is getting a suitable website to display ads for your eCommerce site, and paying them a commission on the sales made by customers they refer to you.

Increasingly, there are now reciprocal agreements between companies. So you might swap an ad in your email with someone else. Ocado and Boden have such a scheme; when you have placed your order on Ocado, the order confirmation screen has an advert for Boden, and together with your groceries the delivery man drops off a co-branded mini Boden catalogue.

Partnerships don't have to be with other eCommerce sites, they might be with forums, newspapers and magazines or even blogs.

How Do I Know Which Marketing Methods Are Important for My eCommerce MasterPlan?

With all the marketing methods that are available, it is necessary to focus on those that will work best for your business. To put you on the fast track to selecting the right ones for your business, I've created this handy table. It highlights the **marketing methods you'd be crazy to ignore**:

	CONTENT	EMAIL	SOCIAL MEDIA	BRAND	OFFLINE	SEARCH	PPC	REMARKETING	PARTNERSHIPS
Online Only	●	●	●	●		●	●	●	
Mail Order		●			●	●		●	
Big Bricks and Clicks		●		●	●	●		●	
Boutique Bricks and Clicks	●	●	●		●	●		●	
Mainstream PiggyBack									●
Niche PiggyBack	●	●	●	●					●
Full MultiChannel		●		●	●	●		●	

So look at your current marketing activity and ask yourself these questions:

1 Which of the key areas for your eCommerce Business Structure are you already doing? How can you do them better?
2 Which aren't you doing? Get started on them now!
3 Finally, which marketing tactics are you using that aren't essential for your eCommerce Business Structure? How are they performing? Should you stop doing them or cut back in order to reinvest the money and effort in the right places?

....

What to Do With All the Research Now it's Done?

Pulling all this information together will give you a great view of where you are right now, and what the next year may hold.

I would really recommend putting it all in one place – be that in a document or in a folder (a real one, or an electronic one) – so that when you need to review your plan, you can easily see what your foundations were. Not only will this save you hours of time in the future, it will also ensure you don't miss anything the next time.

Then take an hour to note the key points from your research ready to create your plan. Your list should include at least:

- KPIs
- good promotions to repeat
- bad promotions
- things we should copy from the competition
- things we need to be aware of
- marketing methods to keep doing
- marketing methods to test
- best customers are…

You may find it useful to put this into a SWOT grid. A SWOT grid outlines your business's internal Strengths and Weaknesses, and the Opportunities and Threats present in the marketplace:

Strengths	**Weaknesses**
Opportunities	**Threats**

Chapter 7 Complete: What's Next?

Following the steps in this chapter, you'll have pulled together all the research (both about your own company and the world outside) that you need to build your marketing plan.

So read on to find out how to do this...

NOTES

What are the key points from this section?

_____

_____

_____

_____

Other notes:

_____

_____

_____

_____

WEBSITE
Visit **eCommerceMasterPlan.com** for more information.

CHAPTER

8

Create Your Marketing Plan

Your marketing plan pulls together everything covered in the book so far.

Before you get cracking with what you've learnt from your research, you need to build a proper marketing plan. An eCommerce marketing plan should include both the channels you are going to use (for example, email, PPC or social media) plus the messages you will be using (for example, sales, promotions, celebrity tie-ins, Father's Day, etc.).

Before we run through HOW to build it, we should consider five things every good marketing plan is.

A Good Marketing Plan is Very Flexible

This is especially so when we are dealing with online marketing activity: in 2011, Pinterest and Google+ barely existed, and now both have over 100 million active members and are driving quality traffic to retailers; in May 2012, Yahoo and Microsoft finally merged their PPC marketing platforms, opening up a viable alternative to Google Adwords for many more UK businesses. Therefore, you have to be ready to change your marketing plan to match shifting online conditions.

Before the plan can change, though, it actually needs to exist. It is so much easier to take advantage of new opportunities if you know what you need to change in order to do so. The best response to this ever-changing marketplace is to be even more rigorous in creating a marketing plan. Not bothering is not an option.

A Good Marketing Plan Considers New and Existing Routes to Market

At the start of the section, we briefly outlined the nine core marketing areas for an eCommerce business and considered which are critical for each eCommerce Business Structure.

Some of these you may already be using and, if they are working, you should keep them. You may not be using others that fit your eCommerce Business Structure, so the new marketing plan should include them, testing them first to make sure they work well enough for you. In online marketing, things are always cropping up and changing, so you just have to keep testing.

A Good Marketing Plan Fits With Your Branding, Your eCommerce Business Structure and Your USP

It seems obvious, but it's worth remembering: if your brand and Unique Selling Point (USP) are focused on customer service, trust and honesty, keep the promotions simple and don't run 'you could win a million' promotions. If you sell personal security products, don't buy cold email data.

Everything you do needs to fit your brand and USP.

A Good Marketing Plan Will Meet Your Objectives

At the core of all eCommerce business objectives are driving sales and new customer acquisition.

Your marketing plan will take a range of activities into consideration to meet those objectives.

A Good Marketing Plan Recognises that You Have Different Types of Customers

From the very first sale, an eCommerce business has two types of customers: those who have bought and those who haven't – also known as your 'buyers' and your 'enquirers'. These different groups of customers need to be marketed to in different ways, because the actions you want each of them to take are different:

- You need **enquirers** to buy for the first time.
- You need **buyers** to buy again.

This is a very simple form of **customer segmentation** and, as your customer database grows, the segmentation will become more complex. Eventually, your customer segmentation will take into account when people buy, what they buy, how much they spend, where they live, their demographic profile, and much more. (See Chapter 9 for more on eCommerce customer segmentation.)

....

Strategy and Tactics, aka Creating the Plan

There are two types of activity we need to put into our marketing plan:

- Do more of your existing activity: more emails, more keywords in Google Adwords, etc.
- Try out some new marketing areas.

During your research, you should have worked out what activity you will continue as per last year, what activity you will invest more effort/money in and what activity you will test or start. Now you can create the plan.

Your marketing plan should be in three formats; this will make it easy to do the activity, monitor the activity and make sure everyone involved knows what is happening. The easier you make it, the more likely it is to happen.

The three formats are:

1 A Calendar of Promotional Activity

This is a month-by-month, or week-by-week, series of activities in each marketing channel. This forms your checklist to make sure everything is happening. If you are struggling to get started, put in what you did last year and the key dates for this year (Christmas, Easter, etc.).

2 A Financial Dashboard

A month-by-month performance tracker that has the cost and sales for each marketing channel AND your KPIs.

3 A Written Guide to the Plan

It doesn't need to be more than a couple of pages but, if you have several people working on implementing the plan, it is critical to keep everything in line.

DOWNLOAD...
Examples of each of these are available on the website at
eCommerceMasterPlan.com/Free

It is usual to work out a full 12-month marketing plan at once, but if that's too daunting, you are only in your first year of trading or you just don't have the time, start with just a six-month or three-month plan. But DON'T FORGET to create the next three months or six months before you get to the end of the first one!

Building Your Plan – Promotional Calendar

Start with the calendar and outline the top events for the year – what big stories/themes will you be focusing on?

- Christmas
- Summer sale
- January sale
- New range
- Easter

Once you've put them all in, are there any gaps? If so, what are you going to fill them with? Maybe a competition? Or a social media growth campaign?

All of this should go on the top few rows of your calendar. Below this add a row for the website's promotional message, and then each marketing method you're going to be using or testing.

On the row of each marketing method (and the website) note what you'll be doing with that marketing each week.

For some channels (like Email), you'll have something happening very frequently. For others (PPC or Remarketing), it might just be notes in one or two weeks of the year about upping budgets or adding ads for new products. This will take some time to create – possibly even a day or two to get it right – but it's well worth it. Once you've got the plan, you'll know exactly what you need to do and when.

	A	B	C	D	E	F	G	H
1	Promo Calendar 201X							
2								
3				January				February
4		1-7	8-14	15-21	22-28	29-4	5-11	12-18
5	World Events				23rd Chinese New Year			14th Valentines
6	Marketing Themes							
7	Promotions							
8	Content							
9	Email							
10	PPC							
11								

Building Your Plan – Financial Targets

Unfortunately, just knowing what marketing we want to do and when isn't enough to keep a business going – we also need to make sure our marketing is driving the sales we need, and the profit too.

This is where the financial plan comes in. Whilst the promotional plan is at a weekly level, the financial plan works best at a monthly level.

You should build up the anticipated sales and costs in each marketing area for each month of the year. Once you've done this – sense check it.

- Are you driving enough sales?
- Do the sales each month look sensible? Are the peaks where they should be?
- Is the ROI there each month?
- Does it meet the objectives?

Don't forget to keep checking back to make sure you're on track and, if not, amend the budget!

	A	B	C	D	E	F	G
1	**Monthly Financial Performance**						
2							
3	**Email**	Sales	Budget	Costs	Budget	ROI	Budget
4	Jan	1,000	900	500	510	100%	76%
5	Feb	1,000	900	500	510	100%	76%
6	Mar	1,000	900	500	510	100%	76%
7	Apr	1,000	900	500	510	100%	76%
8	May	1,000	900	500	510	100%	76%
9	Jun	1,000	900	500	510	100%	76%
10	Jul	1,000	900	500	510	100%	76%
11	Aug	1,000	900	500	510	100%	76%
12	Sep	1,000	900	500	510	100%	76%
13	Oct	1,000	900	500	510	100%	76%
14	Nov	1,000	900	500	510	100%	76%
15	Dec	1,000	900	500	510	100%	76%
16							
17	YTD	12,000	10,800	6,000	6,120	100%	76%
18							
19	**PPC**	Sales	Budget	Costs	Budget	ROI	Budget
20	Jan	1,000	900	500	510	100%	76%

Building Your Plan – Written Guide

I'd suggest not starting on this until you've signed off the calendar and the financial plan.

This is a written guide to your marketing plan for the year – it might even be a video or a presentation! The aim is to have something that adds colour to the spreadsheets, something you can hand to a new team member or a new boss to explain why you're doing the marketing that's planned.

It's also very useful to re-read every couple of months to remind yourself of the big plan!

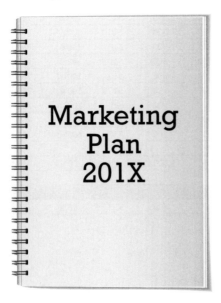

Chapter 8 Complete: What's Next?

Well, now the marketing plan exists, it's time to get implementing! So follow your plan and kick off the first month's activity, but never forget to keep checking and optimising your activity. Read on to find out how to do this...

NOTES

What are the key points from this section?

_____

_____

_____

_____

_____

_____

Other notes:

_____

_____

_____

_____

_____

_____

CHAPTER 9

Test, Measure and Optimise Your Marketing

Marketing requires constant testing, measuring and optimising. What do you need to be aware of when you're doing this? Attribute, segmentation and more...

The most important part of your marketing plan is what happens after you finish writing it.

This is the most important step of all – you MUST regularly **test** new marketing ideas, channels, products, promotions and always **measure** how your marketing plan and those tests are performing. Doing this means that you can get on with the most important part of success in eCommerce – **optimising**. Let's look at each of these in a bit more detail.

Testing

As we learnt in Chapter 7, it's really important to keep on top of all the new marketing methods and opportunities available to you. Simply researching these isn't enough – you need to take the ones that you feel may work for you and test them.

Until you've tested a new idea, you're not going to know it will work for you. No amount of research will conclusively tell you:

- how much traffic that marketing method can drive to your website
- how well that traffic will convert
- what AOV those sales will be at
- how much that traffic is going to cost you – **what it's ROI will be**.

Unless you know all of this you won't know whether or not it's going to work for your business. You can have all the great, crazy, ground-breaking marketing ideas you like, but, if you don't test them, you won't know which to roll out. This also goes for promotional ideas, products, website changes and call centre opening hours – everything in your business.

In the current era of eCommerce, things change very quickly. It's a good bet that the marketing mix you used last year is not the one you'll be using in 12 months' time. So, as marketing methods 'die off', you need to be testing the new options to replenish your traffic. If you're not testing new ideas (in every area of your business), your business will not grow and then it will start to contract.

This might sound a bit extreme, but you should be testing something every single week. Some might be small tests – a different colour for your sale banners, including your brand name in the subject line of your emails, a new Adwords adtext – but you need to see testing as part of the day to day of what you do.

Measuring

With all your existing activity, and all your test activity happening, you need to keep a close eye on performance to see what's working and what isn't. This is where measuring comes in.

I suggest you take a top-down approach. Look at the high level performance of each marketing method first, then delve down into the detail where there are issues, opportunities or you have tests running. This will enable you to look at what you need to, when you need to. At the heart of understanding what is happening is the financial dashboard you created in Chapter 8. This will tell you whether the performance of each marketing channel is good or bad. The key metrics to look at is the ROI, because what you're trying to do is drive traffic to your site and make a profit!

To understand why it's good or bad, you will need to delve deeper and look at the metrics we used to review performance in Chapter 5. Look at the AOV, the conversion rate and the cost per visitor, etc.

For each marketing channel there are different areas to look at. For email marketing, you'll want to look at the open rates, click through rates and how different segments performed. In Google Adwords, delve into the campaigns, adgroups, keywords, adtexts and content network (plus much, much more!).

WEBSITE
If you want to understand how to measure and optimise each individual marketing method, you'll read lots more on the key KPIs for each marketing channel in my book *eCommerce Marketing*, available now at **eCommerceMasterPlan.com**.

You need to be reviewing all these measurements **at least** monthly, and in many areas keep an eye out more regularly than that.

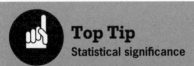

Top Tip
Statistical significance

With any activity you're measuring, you need a certain response to be able to judge whether or not the results are valid. To take an extreme example, if you send an email to a list of 10 people and none of those 10 people buy, does this mean it's a failed email? No. You didn't send it to enough people to properly test it.

This is where statistical significance comes in. So for every test you run, everything you measure, you need to be aware of whether or not the results are statistically significant.

Go to **eCommerceMasterPlan.com/Free** for access to a statistical significance calculator you can use to check your tests.

If you're struggling to run a big enough test to make it statistically significant, here are a few tips:

- Expand the date range – this works especially well with PPC campaigns. If you're not getting statistically significant results looking at seven days of data – look at a month of data, or even longer.
- Re-run the test a few times – with email, if you're testing using your brand name in the subject line, do the same test over three or four sends.

Although not perfect, it's usually possible to find a way to extend a test to make it statistically significant.

Optimisation

Optimisation is the key to all success in your eCommerce business. You should be optimising everything (call centre scripts, website page layouts, products, pricing, customer service standards and, of course, your marketing).

Putting optimisation simply, if something is working well and hitting your ROI targets:

- do more of it, put more resources behind it
- learn why it's doing well and make it even better

If something isn't doing well and is not hitting your ROI targets:

- do less of it
- consider stopping it altogether
- tweak it to make it work for you. Work out which parts of it aren't working and fix them.

As you'll be testing continuously, you're going to be optimising continuously too!

The danger of optimisation is taking it too far. At the end of the day, you have limited resources in time as well as in money. So there is always a level of optimisation where it's not worth your time. For example:

- If you have an email list of under 5,000, then segmenting that list into two and creating a different html email for each segment every time you send just isn't going to be worth the time.
- If in your Google Adwords account you have 50 adgroups that drive fewer than one sale per month, it's not worth testing promotional adtexts in those adgroups.

- If the results you're getting are never going to be statistically significant, then it is not worth spending time on the tests.

....

Taking Your Testing, Measuring and Optimising Further

As you measure performance and amend your marketing channels, promotions, products, website, and more, you'll start to be able to take your segmentation and analysis to the next level. The following are all ways you might want to do this.

Analytics – the Numbers that Are Going to Keep Everything on Track

We need to make sure that the numbers we're looking at are accurate. This means making sure your systems are giving you the right numbers. (Although we're not going to go into it here, this includes the information you are getting from your accountants and from your order processing systems.)

The first thing to get set up properly is your website analytics. Google Analytics is a free package that can be set up very easily and will give you most of what you need to understand your website and marketing performance. There are other analytics tools available. Whichever you choose, make sure they are correctly in place, with:

- every page tagged accurately
- conversion tracking accurately implemented on the order confirmation page, and turned on in Google Analytics.

You'll also find that a lot of your marketing tools have their own conversion tracking that can be implemented; most email marketing systems will have some code to be added to the order confirmation page, as do Google Adwords and Microsoft Adcentre, etc. You will often find it's necessary to set these tracking systems up as well because when you get the conversion data fed back into those tools, it makes it easier to analyse how well they are working. For example, setting up the Google Adwords conversion tracking will show you the orders driven by each keyword and adtext – essential for the optimisation process.

Don't be afraid to set up all the conversion tracking options you have got (it's also very useful for when one of them has a bad day!). Before you start setting them up, though, be clear on what you want the value to be. Most conversion tracking codes allow a real number to be put into the value field (so you'll know if the order was for £5 or £500 – very important!). You need to decide what this number is going to be.

- Including or excluding VAT?
- Including or excluding postage?
- Don't forget to check that your website can handle this!

I would always advise tracking it excluding postage and any discounts. Including or excluding VAT depends on and how you usually look at the sales numbers in your business. Whichever value format you choose, make sure that it's set up in the same way for EVERY piece of tracking code you put in place, and that you always use the same number in your analysis.

Top Tip
Google Analytics set-up tips:

- If you can get the Google Analytics eCommerce tracking set up fully, then you will also get product sales data, which is REALLY useful for quickly seeing which promotions drove sales of which product.
- Do check that the 'This site is an ecommerce site' box is ticked if you are in the process of setting up the tracking! If the box is unticked, it will look as if the tracking isn't working.
- Make sure you have an Admin account; if your login only has 'User' access, ask for this to be changed.
- If you are using Google Adwords, link it with your Google Analytics account: it will give you much better reporting on Adwords' performance.
- Consider setting up a goal for successful catalogue requests or email sign-ups.
- You can create custom dashboards, which are really useful for a quick and easy check of what's going on.
- You can also set any report to automatically email to a set distribution list each month/day/week – VERY useful for keeping people informed and for making sure you don't forget to look at the numbers!
- Google URL Builder is a very simple tool that lets you easily add tracking code to any link into your website, so if you run a promotion with a magazine, you can tag all the links from the magazine back to you, which means you can easily see what traffic does on your site.

WEBSITE
You can find a link to the Google URL Builder Tool at
eCommerceMasterPlan.com/Free

eCommerce Customer Segmentation

The first level of segmentation any eCommerce business should put in place is separating the buyers and the enquirers. It's a great first step to take because you will see an improvement in sales by treating these two segments differently. Plus, it's easy to tell who has and hasn't bought from you, so no matter how simple your systems are, it's almost always possible to segment your database this way.

We treat buyers and enquirers differently because we want them to do different things.

We want the buyers to buy AGAIN.

They have already bought from us once, so we know a lot about them (name, address, email, what they bought, etc.), which means we can market to them much more effectively.

They know us; they have taken the leap of faith and trusted us to provide them with the product/service they wanted and not to do bad things with their data. We have treated them well, and so built up a level of trust with them. So they are already predisposed to trust us (buy from us) again.

We want the enquirers to buy for the first time.

They haven't ever bought from us, we don't know much about them and we might only have their email address, so we can't tailor the marketing to them very precisely. This means we're going to need to make a really compelling offer to get them to take the first leap of faith and buy from us.

On the plus side, though, they do already know about us. (They have visited our website and signed up for an email, responded to an advert or similar.) Not only do they already know about us, they also want to know more about us – so they are ready to listen to what we've got to say.

Segmentation at the simplest level is straightforward to do, and it's easy to see how to treat the different segments and what the likely benefits from that will be.

As you were reading through the buyer and enquirer descriptions, there were probably some questions floating around your head:

- What if they enquired a year ago?
- We ran that competition with X magazine last month and picked up lots of enquirers, but I think they might have been after the prize rather than us – what about these people?
- We have customers who only buy for Valentine's Day – what about them?
- Some of our customers buy in store, phone to order and use the website – what about them?
- Men buy gifts from us at Christmas, but not during the rest of the year. Why?
- We have customers who buy low-priced items from us every month, but others who spend LOTS in one order every six months – should we treat them differently?

All of these are great questions to be asking and show just how much you can do with your segmentation. They also highlight the most difficult thing about segmentation: if you try to implement everything now, you'll drive yourself (or your marketing team) insane. It's too much to do all in one go and, because there is so much going on, you will find it really hard to work out what is actually working and what isn't.

Build Your Segmentation Plan

WORKBOOK
Download the segmentation plan workbook at
eCommerceMasterPlan.com/Free

You need to plan the implementation: in what order are you going to tackle the stages of segmentation? Our outline of the key segmentation options provides you with a checklist of segmentations to use with your data. Start at the top and just work your way through them. Not all will be relevant for your business, so look at the data to work out which you should use and pay attention to.

We have started with the four segmentations that Mail Order businesses have been using for decades to build their businesses effectively: buyers/enquirers and RFM, which stands for recency, frequency, monetary value.

- Buyers *vs* enquirers – a no-brainer, very effective and very easy to do.
- Recency – how recently did they buy/enquire? The more recently someone last interacted with the business, the more likely they are to buy again. Suggest doing this in 6-month to 12-month blocks.
- Frequency – how frequently do they buy? Once a year, three times a year, 10 times a year? You will need to investigate your database to find the right segmentation for this group. As well as trying to get the next purchase, you are aiming to increase their frequency.

- Monetary value – how much do they spend each time they buy? Under £25? £26 to £50? Over £50? Again, you will need to investigate your data to find the right splits for you. Of course, you are also trying to get these customers to spend more with you; if they normally only spend £25, you want them to start spending over £25.

Buyers/enquirers plus RFM forms a very solid foundation for your segmentation. You should map your customers in these segmentations in a matrix like the one below in order to see where the clumps of data are.

	A	B	C	D	E	F	G	H
1	**RFM Example Grid**							
2	each white cell would contain the number of people in that segment							
3								
4	Only purchased once							
5	Last Order>	0-6m	7-12m	13-18m	19-24m	25-36m	37-42m	42m+
6	AOV							
7	£0-30							
8	£30-60							
9	£60-100							
10	£100+							
11								
12	Purchased twice							
13	Last Order>	0-6m	7-12m	13-18m	19-24m	25-36m	37-42m	42m+
14	AOV							
15	£0-30							
16	£30-60							
17	£60-100							
18	£100+							
19								
20	Purchased three times							
21	Last Order>	0-6m	7-12m	13-18m	19-24m	25-36m	37-42m	42m+
22	AOV							
23	£0-30							
24	£30-60							
25	£60-100							
26	£100+							

DOWNLOAD...
You can download an Excel version of this from
eCommerceMasterPlan.com/Free

Other segmentation options

These look more deeply at buyer behaviour:

- Source of the data – this is really useful with enquirer data because it will show you which of your enquiry generation methods capture the best data. (Was that magazine competition worth it? Or was the small advert in the Sunday Times better?) It's also really good to continue to track this once they become buyers, because then you know where your best buyers come from.
- Seasonality – when they buy, do they only buy at Christmas or only in the summer? In which case, you either only market to them when they buy OR you need to try to convert them to buyers outside the key season.
- Products – which items in your range do they buy? Jewellery or furniture? The vacuum cleaner or just the vacuum bags?
- Purchase type – are they buying for themselves or as a gift?
- Multichannel – does the customer use all your channels to buy, or just one?
- Marketing response – you can't track this in every channel, but with email you can track who is opening and who is clicking your emails.
- Customer service usage – are they a 'good' or a 'bad' customer? This could also be returns rate or cancelled orders information.
- GeoDemographics – male or female, age, where in the country, MOSAIC profiling or similar.

With all this segmentation, you should always be asking the following:

- Which segments make up the best customers, and how do you keep them?

- Which segments make up the worst customers – and is it worth marketing to them at all? (Is someone who only ever spends £10 and orders only once a year worth the marketing expense?)
- Is our segmentation structure right? Should we go into more detail, or less?

Attribution

A big debate in eCommerce at the moment is how you should attribute sales back to the marketing channels involved. During the work-up to an order, one customer may have visited your site many times via several different routes. For example:

Magazine website > email > 'red widget' PPC > brand PPC > affiliate > PURCHASE

Which Route Deserves the Credit for the Sale?

Traditionally, attribution has been done on a 'last click wins' model – so whatever marketing was tracked driving the customer to the website just before the sale gets the sale. But this gives a skewed view of marketing performance; in the above example, your PR, email and PPC get no credit.

This also gets very complicated when you take offline activity into account. Imagine the customer also received a catalogue from you, or went into a store: how do you reward the store and the catalogue for their impact on the sale? How do you know they had an impact?

As yet, there is no clear route to track the impact of offline marketing, and most companies stick with the imperfect 'last click wins' because it's the easiest to do – it's what Google Analytics automatically does.

If you choose to do this too, be aware that the other tracking codes on your website (the email one, the PPC one) will report complete data, so everyone influenced by an email will be reported back to the email tool. So, if you take performance reports direct from those tools, you will count some sales twice.

Customer Lifetime Value – Taking Your Business to the Next Level of Profitability

This combines both attribution and segmentation, taking them to a whole other level.

The aims of your marketing plan and your customer segmentation are to find the most effective way to meet your ROI and volume targets. At the absolute centre of getting this right is knowing that your marketing spend is going to the right places. The customer segmentation exercise will help you to work out how you can increase average order values (AOVs) and which customers to focus on, but to really make the whole system sing you need to understand your customer lifetime value (CLV).

CLV is the amount a person will spend with you in their lifetime, minus the amount you spent servicing that customer. So it's basically the profit you will get from each customer. It's an amazing number to know.

If your overall CLV is £100, you know you can spend up to £99 to recruit a customer and you will turn a profit. But not all customers are going to have a positive CLV...

Now, this is where CLV becomes really exciting! Once you are able to work out CLV at customer level, you can plug it into your segmentation model. This enables you to see:

- the profitability of each segment – and some segments won't be profitable. For some segments, you should cut back on your marketing and focus that marketing on moving them into another segment. For example, get them to order via more channels, more frequently, at a higher AOV, etc.
- how much you can afford to spend to recruit the right types of customer, because you have tracked the source of the data so you can see CLV by data source
- which segments you should do MORE marketing to in order to move them into better segments, or to increase their profit even more.

Work Out Your CLV

In an ideal world, you would be able to divide every cost in the business accurately to each order you process and allocate each order back to a customer. Achieving this would change every process in the business and keep a bevy of analysts in work for months. There is a way to do it more quickly in order to get the benefits faster (and of course you might later choose to make it more complex), so just start with a 12-month CLV:

- Take all your costs for the last 12 months.
- Divide by the number of orders you processed in the last 12 months.

- Now you have your total cost per order (hopefully it is lower than your AOV!).
- Divide the number of orders you had last year by the number of people who bought from you last year: this is your average orders per customer.
- Multiply your AOV by the average orders per customer: this gives you your average spend per customer.
- Subtract your total cost per order from your average spend per customer: this gives you your 12-month CLV.

(The next step towards a true CLV is to take the marketing spend out and allocate that back to each customer, for example if each email sent costs 20p, a customer should get 'charged' 20p for each email they receive.)

Hopefully, you can see here the power of understanding your CLV. Here are a few common CLV findings to get you started:

- A customer who buys via two channels (shop and web) is worth twice what a customer who buys via one channel is worth.
- A customer who doesn't shop seasonally (they shop with you all year round) is worth more than a customer who does.
- There will be one very expensive (per first order) recruitment tool (that you have probably stopped using) that only ever brought in profitable customers.
- Is frequency of order or value of order the most powerful for your profits?

Chapter 9 Complete: What's Next?

- However you choose to do it in your business, you need to be testing, measuring and optimising your marketing activity at every level – messages, keywords, headlines, channel *vs* channel, segment *vs* segment.
- This needs to be part of what you do day in day out – testing, measuring and optimising are business as usual.
- Always, always test, test, test.

NOTES

What are the key points from this section?

_____

_____

_____

_____

_____

Other notes:

_____

_____

_____

_____

_____

Step 3: I Have Built It: Why Haven't They Come? (aka Marketing!) and *eCommerce MasterPlan* Complete: What's Next?

Congratulations! You have now completed the 3 Steps to building your eCommerce MasterPlan.

What Sort of eCommerce Business Are You?
- Identify your eCommerce Business Structure
- Identify the Scale of Your Product Range
- Differentiate your Business

Establishing The Core Foundations
- Build the Right Website
- Build your Business for Profit and Growth
- Select your Products and Promotions

I Have Built It: Why haven't they come? (aka Marketing!)
- Research your Marketing Plan
- Creating your Marketing Plan
- Test, Measure and Optimise your Marketing

This is only the start of your eCommerce journey. The power of your MasterPlan lies in you constantly optimising what you are doing: optimising the website, the products, the finances, the marketing.

Whenever there is an important decision to be made, don't forget to ask yourself:

- 'Does this fit with my eCommerce Business Structure?'
- 'Does this change my Product Range Scale (PRS)?'
- 'Does this help build my USP?'

Next Steps

WEBSITE
- Visit **eCommerceMasterPlan.com** for more information on all areas of the *eCommerce MasterPlan*.
- Don't forget to sign up for the emails from **eCommerceMasterPlan.com** to make sure you get the latest news of what's happening in eCommerce straight into your inbox.
- I hope you have found the contents of this book useful, and I would love to hear your thoughts. Just go to **eCommerceMasterPlan.com** and you'll find lots of ways to let me know.
- If you want to fast-track your progress, check out the 'Fast-track' options on the website.

You've Read the Book, What's Next?

. . . .

You have now built your own eCommerce MasterPlan, so it's time to start implementing. But it's not time to stop learning – eCommerce and online marketing are still evolving so:

- always keep optimising – optimise your products, your website, your financials and, of course, your marketing
- keep learning – watch out for new opportunities, and test those you think might work for your business.

I am committed to keeping **eCommerceMasterPlan.com** up to date with the information the eCommerce business owner or marketer needs to know. It is simple, sensible advice. Visit today, subscribe to our emails and follow us on social media.

The *eCommerce MasterPlan* is the first in a series of books that help eCommerce businesses improve and grow. Why not commit to continue to learn right now and order one of the other books in the series today from **eCommerceMasterPlan.com** or Amazon?

- *eCommerce Marketing: How to Drive Traffic that Buys to Your Website*
- *eCommerce Social Media: How to Run Your Social Media Effectively and Efficiently!*

Contact Us

. . . .

If you want more help, or want to accelerate your progress even faster…

- Take a look on **eCommerceMasterPlan.com** for our training and inner circle programmes.
- Chloë is available to speak or consult right now – contact details are given below.
- On the website we have details of where Chloë is speaking in the coming months.
- Chloë's online marketing agency, indiumonline, can help you with a range of managed online marketing activity. See **indiumonline. co.uk**.
- Plus, you'll find lots of great extra content on **eCommerceMasterPlan.com**

Contact details:

t: 01865 980 616 or 01872 888 737
e: chloe@ecommercemasterplan.com
p: eCommerce MasterPlan
Windsor House
12–14 High St
Kidlington
OX5 2DH

Recommended Reading

. . . .

I have found the following eCommerce-related books both enlightening and enjoyable – these are the ones I don't lend to anyone!

Anderson, Chris, *The Long Tail* (Hyperion Books, 2006)

A concept that you need to understand if you are going to succeed online, and so well explained. Read this and you'll see the long tail everywhere.

Collier, Paul, M., *Accounting for Managers: Interpreting Accounting Information for Decision-Making* (John Wiley & Sons, 2012)

If you struggle with the numbers, this is the book for you.

Godin, Seth, *Poke the Box* (The Domino Project, 2011)

This takes only about two hours to read cover to cover and it's Seth's manifesto for getting on with it, for initiating. It will be on my Kindle forever.

Malmsten, Ernst, *Boo Hoo: A Dot.com Story From Concept to Catastrophe* (Random House, 2002)

The ultimate tale of eCommerce woe. This might have all happened over 10 years ago, but many companies are still making the same mistakes today.

Timpson, John, *Upside Down Management: A Common Sense Guide to Better Business* (John Wiley & Sons, 2010)

This is a very good guide to retailing, with a pragmatic, sensible approach.

Find out more on **eCommerceMasterPlan.com**

I'm already building up more content about the different eCommerce Business Structures and news from the ever-changing world of eCommerce on the website – so visit today to subscribe:

eCommerceMasterPlan.com (including RSS Feed and Email Newsletter).

Go on, sign up for more at **eCommerceMasterPlan.com**